Virginia Land Patents
Of The Counties Of
Norfolk, Princess Anne & Warwick
From Patent Books
"O" & "6" - 1666 to 1679

Transcribed & Edited by

Alice Granbery Walter

CLEARFIELD

Reprinted for Clearfield Company by
Genealogical Publishing Company
Baltimore, Maryland
1993, 2011

ISBN 978-0-8063-5089-9

Made in the United States of America

This volume is an index (abstract) of patents in which the county is not given. The actual patents are recorded in the appropriate patent books.

There are 191 pages on this microfilm. The writer has abstracted all of those which were of interest and which might possibly pertain to Lower Norfolk, Norfolk, Princess Anne and Warwick Counties.

The microfilm was obtained from the Virginia State Library in Richmond, Virginia.

Virginia State Land Office - Counties O
Reel 321 - 31 feet

Abstracted

by

Alice Granbery Walter

ABBREVIATIONS:

Afsd   = aforesaid   sd = said
mkd   = marked   th = then or thence
p   = per, pro &c   Trans: = transportation
Pat: & Patt = patent   VSL = Virginia State Library
po   = pole (land measure)   wch = which
pson   = person y^t = yet, sometimes that
pt & pte = part   xxx = illegible or missing
// = parenthesis in the record   ( ) = supplied by the editor

Nugent - Cavaliers & Pioneers by Nell Marion Nugent, reprint 1963.

ABRAHAM TURNER   page 21

Patent Book 1 p 828 - 10 Oct 1642 - 200 acres lying in Mook Jack bays
in the river that lyeth in the North East side of Ware River. (see
Nugent p 135: 200 acres in Mock Jack Bay same date - NE side of Ware
River, adj. WILLIAM DEBNAM, RICHARD CREEDLE & TURNERS CREEK. 100 acs.
for the per. adv. of himself twice, and 100 acs. for trans. of 2 pers.
ROBERT CARDE & THOMAS HARTE.)

DANIELL LEWELLYN   page 22

Patent Book 1 p 845 - 10 Oct 1642 - 856 acres. The Northermost part
beg: above MRS. HEYMAN N on the upper branches of TURKEY ISLAND CREEK.
(see Nugent p 135:   Daniell Lewellyn, Gent., 856 acs same as above
& S on the head of MR. ASTONS land. The Southermost part extending on
Mr. Aston & W upon JOSEPH ROYALL bet..DOCKMANS CREEK & SHERLY HUNDRED.
Trans. of 17 Pers: MICHAELL PEACOCK, CHARLES EDGAR, THO: MORGAN, JAMES
FOSTER, ROBERT HOPPS, TEGO FRAYLE, HEN: HITCHCOX, ROBERT WARD, THO:
RICHARDSON, THO: TAYLOR, MARKE CHETON, MARY DAVIS, JOHN TALBOTT, JOHN
DEVALL, ROBERT HALLOME, FRANCES HALLOME, ELIZA: JACKSON. The date is
given in Nugent as 27 Oct 1642.)

CHRISTOPHER BOYCE   page 24

Patent Book 1 p 870 - 21 Jan 1642/3 - 2000 acres. (see Nugent p 142:
which gives date as 21 Dec 1642...in PEANKATANKE RIVER about 3 mi. up
the S side at plumtree point. The following names appear under this
record: JOHN CRISPE, WM: VENICE, JON: JOHNSON, CHRIST: BOYCE, MORDE-
CAY COOKE, JON: TIPLAD, JON: FELLS, JAS: GREENWILL, JON: BARLOW,
WALTER BRACE (Bruce?), KATH: LEWIS, JON: WILLIAMS, JON: WITHERS, EDMD:
PORTER & UX (wife), EDMD: PORTER JUNR:, JON: PORTER JUNR:, JON: PORTER
SENR: MARMADUKE ATKINSON, MANASSA PORTER, ELIZ: FLOWERDEW, THOMAS SIMP-
SON, RICHARD WILLIAMS, ROBERT FENTRICE, JON: CARRAWAY, ROBERT FENTRICE,
GEORG HARLAND, JARMAN CONNAWAY, THOMAS BLATT, RICH: WOOTTON, ANNE MAR-
SHALL, THO: KEMP, JOHN OLIVER, THO: COOPER, THOMAS PITCHERD, THO: CORR-
ELL (Sorrell), JOYCE STONE, JOHN CANNADAY, WILLIAM JACKSON, JOHN NEMO
(Nimmo?)

RANDALL HOLT   page 24

Patent Book 1 p 880 - 1 Aug 1643 - sonn and lawful heire of MARY BAYL-
EY late of HOGG ISLAND sole dau & heir of JOHN BAYLEY of sd Island.
(see Nugent p 143 to continue: 700 acs called HOGG IS. lying over a-
gainst ARCHERS HOPE on the TAPPAHANNA side of the river & 10 acs in
JAMES ISLAND adj. the late dwelling howse of ROBERT EPERS, towards
GOOSE HILL, N towards land lately belonging to WILLIAM FAIRFAX & W
upon land lately belonging to JENKIN ANDREWES. 490 acres being express-
ly granted to the sd. MARY BAYLEY by the name of MARY BAYLEY ORPHANT,

20 Feb 1619, with the special clause & privisoe that if upon due survey
hereafter to be made the sd. island doe not amount to 490 acres that so
much as it wanteth shall be supplyed to the said MARY BAYLEY in some
other place and if the said Island doe conteyne above 490 acres that
then the said Mary doe purchase the Surplusage from the Company, tec.
The surplus being 210 acs. is now due by trans. of 5 servts. in the shipp
"William and Thomas" 24 Aug 1618 by JOHN BAYLEY: HUGH PRICE, WILLIAM
DONE (or Dove), PHILLIPP ROPER, HENRY BROUGHTON, ROBERT REDDINGS.)

JOHN CALVERT   page 34

Patent Book 1 p 899 - 2 Sep 1643 - 300 acres: brother & heire of Doct:
GEORGE CALVERT decd. (Pat was afterwards renewed in the name of ANTHONY
ELLIOTT 24 Jul 1645) 300 acres begg: at a swampe or small branch that
issueth out of POINT COMFORT CREEKE (Nugent p 146 - a swamp dividing
this land from that of NICHOLAS ROE, commonly called BUCK ROWE........)

BARTHOLOMEW HOSKINS   page 29

Patent Book 2 p 172 - 1 Jan 1648 - 1350 acres on Rappahannock River, Swd
(same renewed 12 Aug 1651 - see Nugent p 219) side of.   (see Nugent
p 182 - same patent: for trans. of 27 persons: MR. BARTH: HOSKINS 5
times, 6 negroes, RICHARD HARWAY, RICHARD FOSTER 2 times, RICHD: WINTER,
ABRA: THOMAS, RICHAD: HOLMES, RICHARD SYMONDS, FRA: WHITE, MARGARY
SMITH, ANDREW EDWARDS.)

JOHN DENNIS   page 30

Patent Book 2 p 177 - 15 Oct 1649 - 350 acres at Great WICOCOMOCO RIVER
bounded on the Northern parts with a branch of the sd river...(see Nugent p 183. head rights are given)

JOHN SENEOR   page 31

Patent Book 2 p 207 - 9 Apr 1650 - 100 acres on the S side of JAMES
RIVER a little above the Colledge.   (see Nugent p 190)

                                                               page 44

    The following is a list of names of the persons with the quantity to
each name only. See a Memo concerning the same made on the records of
Patent Book 2 p 369) (see also p 226 in Nugent for a little fuller
explanation)

SAMUELL ABBOTT 25 po fol 80   THOMAS HORNE 100 acs fol 5
THOMAS CAWSEY 100 acs fol 20   JOHN WATKINS 200 acs fol 5
EDWARD DOUGLAS   JOHN YARTES 250 acs fol 5
            1100 acs fol 20
(Patent Book 2 p 5 has date 1643 & p 20 - 1644 & P 80 - 1646 see Nugent)

JOHN DEBAR   page 45

Patent Book 3 p 2 - 6 Oct 1653 (Nugent gives 6 Nov 1653)- 200 acres
in the WESTERN BRANCH of ELIZA: RIVER on the North side of ye branch
(Nugent p 228: beg at a point by a small creek side, running NW &
joining to THOMAS WRIGHTS land, etc., and up BROAD CREEK to the land
of RICHARD STARLINGE. Trans. of 4 pers: HEN: CLARKE, FRA: PEIRCEY,
ANN ARCHER, JAMES ROE.) see also (Nugent p 297 - same patent 6 Oct
1654 PB 3 p 298, Granted unto sd Debarr 6 Nov 1653 and since proved
deserted land, as appears by order of the County Court of Low. Norf.
21 Sep 1654)

LT: COL: JOHN CHEESEMAN ESQR & JOHN ADLESTON   page 45

Patent Book 3 p 10 - 13 May 1654 - 300 acs: lying on the North side
of CHEESEMANS CREEK (Chas.Riv.Co?) & on the BAY TREE NECK (Jas.City
Co.?) &c (Nugent p 232 continues... beg. at corner tree of JOHN ADLE-
STONS devdt. running by marked trees being the deviding line bet. sd.
CHEESEMAN & ADLESTONE & land of MR. BEALE & JOHN CLERKSON &c. Trans:
of 6 pers: JON: WOODHOUSE, HEN: MIDLUX, JON: BINKS, THO: PEALES, JON:
ANDERSON, MARY STREATLY, JOHN _______(land due for))

ROBERT CAPPS & ROBERT SPRING   page 46

Patent Book 3 p 17 - 3 May 1653 - 300 acres situate in WESTERN BRANCH
of ELIZA: RIVER joining to ..... RIGLESWORTH land. (Nugent p 236
gives Trans: of 6 pers: RICHD: HALLAWAY, JON: JACKSON, ROBT: CAPPS,
ROBT: SPRINGE, PABLE KINGLE, JON: GREGMAN.)

HUMPHREY EDEY   page 46

Patent Book 3 p 18 - 27 Dec 1652 - 250 acres on the NW branch of
NANSEMOND RIVER joining to the land of MR. ROBERT LAWRENCE. (Nugent
p 236 gives: Trans: of 5 pers: HUM: EDEY & his wife, JOAN BARNES,
WM: BARLOW, ELIZ: HARWOOD.

RICHARD PINNER   page 60

Patent Book 3 p 242 - 20 Apr 1653 - 150 acres lying in ELIZABETH RIV:
between the two MAINE BRANCHES OF CHURCH CREEK..(Nugent p 285:.......
bounded from the TIMBER NECK SWAMP along the Northermost main branch
of the creek NE thence SE parallel to the GREAT SWAMP &c. Trans. of
3 pers: RICHARD PINNER, SARAH TERRY, MILICENT SIMONS.) (Note: Is
this PINNER's POINT? AGW)

THOMAS DEYNES   page 64

Patent Book 3 p 323 - 6 Jun 1654 - 500 acres on a Creek called DEEP
CREEK being a branch of the SOUTHERN BRANCH of ELIZA: RIVER. (Nugent
p 303: Trans. of 10 pers: MARY JACKSON, EDW. DENSE (Deynes?) ROBERT
MEAL, JOAN PORTER, THOMAS POTTER, EDWARD BARNES, HUMPHREY HAGGIST,
ELIZABETH TOWERS, ELIZABETH BEVIS, ELIZABETH MATHY.)

RICHARD FOSTER   page 64

Patent Book 3 p 336 - 1 Apr 1655 - 200 acres on the head of the Sout-
herd Creek in SEVERNE in Mockjack bay..(Nugent p 306: ...adj. Col.
LUDLOW. Trans of 4 pers: ELLEN FOSTER, MARY FOSTER, SARAH DAVIS,
ROBT: BYNAM, FRA: BIGNALL.)

GEORGE KEMPE   page 69

Patent Book 4 p 37 - 26 Mar 1656 - 400 acres in LYNNHAVEN PARISH beg:
at COL: SIDNEYS now in possession of JOHN PORTER SENR. (Nugent p 328:
Due by virtue of the rights of a patent granted him 28 Apr 1652.)

JAMES TURNER   page 87

Patent Book 4 p 515 - 20 Oct 1661 (Nugent gives 9 Jul 1653)- 800 acres
on the South side of YORK RIVER in the Narrows joining to the land of
MR. CROSHAW (RAMSHAW?) & JOHN BUTTLER.

ROGER WILLIAMS(ON?)   page 93

Patent Book 4 p 590 - 25 Sep 1663 - 350 acres on the Northern side of
the RIVER CAROLINE.(Same page Book "O" - P84 p 591 see later) (Nugent
p 427 Trans of 7 pers: MAN: ROGERS, THOS: JONES, THO: JEFFRIES, JOHN
ROSSE, CHA: SEWARD, JNO: DANIELL, JONE ROPER. Same page Book "O":

MR. JOHN HARVEY - Patent Book 4 p 590 - 25 Sep 1663 - 350 acres on the
Northern side of the RIVER CAROLINA beg: by ROGER WILLIAMS'S land,
Nugent p 427: running down same to the miles end of sd WILLIAMS &c.
same date.)

JOHN CARTWRIGHT   page 103

Patent Book 5 p 160 - 14 Jul 1664 - 100 acres on the South Side in the
EASTERN BRANCH in ELIZA: RIVER bounding on the Easter(n) side of HENRY
NICHOLLS line. (Nugent p 471 gives: S side of E Br of Eliza: Riv.
bounding on E side of Henry Nicholls)

RICHARD YATES (YEATES)   page 121

Patent Book 6 p   - 13 Mar 1667/8 - 450 acres on the SOUTHERN BR.
of ELIZABETH RIVER being a parcel of land lying between the land of
ffRANCIS SAWYER (SAYER) and his own land. (Nugent ends with PB 5)

COL: LEMUEL MASON   page 128

Patent Book 6 p 674 - 24 Apr 1679 - 1250 acres beg. at a point called
HOG PEN POINT which lyeth on the SW side of the Creek that divides
this land & ye land of THO: WILLOUGHBY.

GEORGE SPIVIE   page 130

Patent Book 7 p 89 - 20 Apr 1681 - 400 acres in the UPPER PARISH OF
NANZEMUND adjoining land of JAMES PETERS.

MATHEW SPIVEY   . page 134

Patent Book 7 p 259 - 10 Apr 1683 - 200 acres in the UPPER PARISH OF
NANSIMOND beg: &c by or nigh the CYPRESS SWAMP.

MATHEW SPIVIE   page 131

Patent Book 7 p 91 - 20 Apr 1681 - 86 acres in the UPPER PARISH of
NANZEMUNT beg. &c on the So. side of a Br. that runs up behind EDW:
HOLMES.

NOTE: In Patent Book "O" there are many patents which are mostly in
NANSEMOND COUNTY in the Patent Books numbered 6, 7, & 8. AGW.

JOEL MARTIN   page 142

Patent Book 8 p 45 - WILLIAM HILLIARD 21 Apr 1690 - 200 acres lately
belonging to JOEL MARTIN & now in possession of sd HILLIARD in LYNN-
HAVEN PARISH Escheated from Thomas ALLEN.

THOMAS SCOTT   page 141

Patent Book 8 p 14 - 20 Oct 1689 - 150 acres in the WESTERN BRANCH of
ELIZA: RIVER joining to land of CAPT: JOHN SIPSEY.
Patent Book 8 p 15 - 20 Oct 1689-150 acres in ELIZABETH RIVER between
(the) two MAINE BRANCHES OF CHURCH CREEK.

HUGH CAMPBELL   page 143

Patent Book 8 p 226 - 29 Apr 1692 - 200 acres at the head of a Creeke
called JULIAN CREEK being a br. of the So. Br. of ELIZA: RIVER.

JAMES THELABELL of Norfolk   page 144

Patent Book 8 p 448 - 20 Apr 1694 - 423 Acres in LITTLE CREEK PRECINCT
adjoining to a place called WOLFES NECK.

JOHN BOWERS of Norfolk County   page 146

Patent Book 9 p 47 - 29 Oct 1696 - 166 acres being part of a patent of
400 acres of land to THO: MEARS dated 1 Jun 1649 on the NWward side of
the WESTERN BRANCH of ELIZA: RIVER. (see Nugent p 182)

GEORGE TURNER   page 147

Patent Book 9 p 250 - 24 Apr 1700 - 800 acres on the South side of
YORK RIVER in the NARROWS.

JOHN MARKHAM   page 185

Patent Book Y p 335 - 13 Apr 1786 - 804 Acres on the North side of
BANISTER RIVER begin: on the DRY BRANCH.

Rogers, Man: 4
Roper, Jone   4
            Phillipp   2
Rosse, John   4
Sawyer, Francis   (Sayer)   5
Sayer, Francis   (Sawyer)   5
Scott, Thomas   5
Seneor, John   (Lanier?)   2
Seward, Cha: 4
Sidney, Col   (John?)   4
Sipsey, Capt. John   5
Smith, Margery   2
Sorrell, Thomas (Correll?)   1
Spivie (Spivey), George   5
                Mathew   5
Spring, Robert   3
Starlinge, Richard   3
Streatly, Mary   3
Symonds, Richard   2
Talbott, John   1
Taylor, Thomas   1
Thelaball, James   6
Thomas, Abra: 2
Thurmer?, George   6
            James   4
Towers, Elizabeth   4
Turner, Abraham   (Thurmer?)   1
            George   "   6
            James   "   4
Ward, Robert   1
Watkins, John   2
White, Fra: 2
Williams(on?), Roger   4
Willoughby, Thomas   5
Winter, Richard   2
Woodhouse, Jon: 3
Wrights, Thomas   (Wright?)   3
Yartes, John   (Yates)   2
Yates, Richard   5

PLACE & SUBJECT

Archer's Hope   1
Banister River   6
Bay Tree Neck   3
Broad Creek (nr Western Br.)   3
Buck Roe   2
Carolina River   4
Cheeseman's Creek   3
Church Creek   3, 5
Cypress Swamp   5

Deep Creek   4
Dismal Swamp?   3
Dry Branch   6
Eastern Branch, South side of   4
Hog Pen Point   5
Hogg Island   (James River)   1
James River, South side of   2
Julians Creek   5
Little Creek Precinct   6
Lynnhaven Parish   5
Masons Creek?   5
Mock Jack Baye   1,   4
Nansemond County [3]   5
Nansemond River   3
Narrows, in York River   6
Peankatanke River   1
Pinners Point   3
Point Comfort Creek   2
Rappahannock River   2
Schools   2
Severne (River?)   4
Sherly Hundred (Shirley?)   1
Ships: William & Thomas   2
Southern Branch of Eliza. Riv.[2]   5
Timber Neck Swamp   3
Turkey Island Creek (Henrico?)   1
Ware River   1
Western Branch of Eliza. Riv. 3[2],5
                                      6
William & Mary College   2
Great Wieosomoco   2
Wolfes Neck   6
York River   4
          , South side of   6

LOWER NORFOLK COUNTY & WARWICK COUNTY PATENTS

Transcribed

From PATENT BOOK NUMBER 6
1666 - 1679
&
Edited

by

ALICE GRANBERY WALTER

Including
A Few Short Abstracts From Other Counties
which
Were of Interest to the Editor

Transcribed
from
A Microfilm of

THE ORIGINAL PATENT BOOK NUMBER 6

(Land Office Reel 6)

Virginia State Library
Richmond, Virginia

i

In the event any reader wishes to look up the original patents, the page numbers of Patent Book Six are listed directly under the date on each patent. The index also refers to the original book rather than the page numbers of this book.

Examples of the Court Script are reproduced of many names which seemed questionable, and to assist anyone who may turn to the original.

The patents do not run entirely chronologically. The Court Clerks used empty spaces on pages to fill in patents much later than others on the same page. Paper was apparently scarce in the seventeenth century.

This publication has a double purpose which may explain why only the Lower Norfolk and Warwick County patents were transcribed. There are a few short abstracts of other county patents which were of genealogical interest to your editor. First: To accomplish the publication of the Lower Norfolk and Warwick County records. Other Lower Norfolk and Warwick County Records are being prepared for publication at a future date. Secondly: To facilitate the charting of a 17th Century Map of Lower Norfolk County showing the early land owners which will be published at a later date.

The original misspelling in the records has been followed as far as was practical. Many words have probably been spelled correctly, entirely accidentally, it is feared. These are the extent of my errors, it is fervantly hoped, however, that is only wishful thinking for I do not claim to be infallible. The transcript has been double checked, as has the patent book.

ABBREVIATIONS:

Afsd = aforesaid		sd = said	
mkd = marked		th = then or thence	
p = per, pro &c		Trans: = transportation	
Pat: & Patt = patent		VSL = Virginia State Library	
po = pole (land measure)		wch = which	
pson = person		y^t = y.et, sometimes that	
pt & pte = part		xxx = illegible or missing	
// = parenthesis in the record		() = supplied by the editor	

Nugent = Cavaliers & Pioneers by Nell Marion Nugent, reprint 1963.

20 Oct 1666 - RICHARD HEABERD xxx acres of land co. of Westmoreland
    (p2)   (Part of this patent is missing) formerly granted unto
MR. THO: -(missing)- 1661 (or 1662) and by sd. POPE assigned xxxxxxx

26 Oct 1666 - RICHARD BUTT 200 acres in Lower Norfolk County at ye
    (p5)   head of ROBERT BUTT his grant (bounds are given) begin
               at a marked white oake standing by the CYPRUS SWAMP &
runing along the Swamp side E by N........bounding on ANTHONY BEN-
FORD's mkd trees to ROBERT BUTT his line & so bounding on ROBT:
BUTT's line........for trans: of 4 persons: EDWARD HOLT, EDW: WARD-
ING, RICH: KEE and RICE DELL.

30 Oct 1666   THOMAS ffULCHER 200 acres in Lower Norfolk County. sd.
   (p6)   land being formerly granted unto HENRY WAKE decd. and
               lately found to escheat to his Maties..................
now granted unto sd ffulcher.....................................

29 Mar 1668 - FRANCIS MASON and MARY CORE (GORE?) headrights in Pat.
   (p11)   to PETER PRESTLY in Northumberland County.

27 Mar 1656 or 1658 - RICH: HEABEARD 250 acres in Westmoreland County
   (p15a)   and by him deserted................................
24 Oct 1666 granted to JOHN BEARE.

16 Apr 1667 - ROBT: TOWMOND (could this be Robert Thurmer?) 600 acres
   (p24)   lying in County of Charles River .....called MARTEAWS
               Creek.......Charles River.......the sd. devident of ...
               (can't read)- granted unto ffRANCIS TOWMEND the 10th of
Mxx xxxxxxxxx TOWMEND by Patent dated the xxxxxxxxx ROBT: now of right
descends unto the said MR. -(faded)- TOWMEND true and lawful heire to
ye sd ffRANCIS decd.   (It seems that Robert is the descendant of the
sd. ffRANCIS) (The name is definitely not Townsend. AGW)

7 Mar 1666/7 - RICHARD BONNEY 660 acres in Lower Norfolk County.......
   (p31a)   formerly granted unto WM: JACOB decd.......escheated....
               No bounds given.

9 Nov 1666 - JNO: WILLOUGHBY, THO: LANGLEY et als headrights in Patent
   (p35)   to ALEXANDER WILLIAMS in Accomac County.

9 Nov 1666 - IDALY HOSKINS headright in patent to JOHN JENKINS for
   (p36)   land in Accomac County. (most names are hard to read)

7 Mar 1666/7 - PLUMMER BRAY 350 acres in Lower Norfolk County...sd land
   (p37)   being formerly granted to JOHN KEMP.........escheated to
               his Maties.............(no bounds given)

22 Oct 1666 - GEORGE SPIVEY 150 acres in county of Nansemond (can't read
   (p40)   most of this)

21 Aug 1667 - WILLIAM PORTEN 449 acres & 12 pole lying upon the North
   (p47)   side of the Eastern Branch of Elizabeth River in County
                of Lower Norfolk beg: at a mked pine upon a poynt hard
by a Creek side running 226 po East & by South by the River side to a
pine standing upon a small poynt by a gutt joyning to the West side of
ARTHUR TOPPIN's land thence 320 po N & by W into the woods to a pine
on the swamp thence 276 po W by N to ye head of the Creek aforsd & th:
310 po to the first station. For trans: of 9 persons: ISAAC SCOTT,
HENRY WESTON, EDW: SNEALE, JAMES BIRD, THO: DAVIS, SAM'L: WARREN, rest
of names impossible to read.

7 Apr 1671 - GEORGE POOLE, RICHARD FARTHINGALE, RICHARD BARRINGHAM, &
   (p53)   JAMES FARFILD? 800 acres in Gloster Co. in Ware Parish
                ....600 acres formerly branted to HENRY CARBILL by
Pat: dated 6 Mar 1653 & by him assigned to sd POOLE et als & 200 acres
the overplus within the bounds is now due to them for trans: of 4 persons: names not given.

24 Sep 1667 - JNO: WILSON 100 acres of land ......part of 1100 acres
   (p54)   a long and involved change of ownership.....WM: CLARKE
                sould LEONARD LAUGHTON who sold to SETH WARD. Widow
DOROTHY CLARKE mentioned &c.........(County is not given but VARINA is
mentioned.

6 Nov 1673 - COLL: JOHN STRINGER 1050 acres in Accomac County.......
   (p64)   mkd trees of COLL: KENDALLS land.......HENRY SMITHS land
                .....due for trans: of 21 persons: ELIZABETH CARVER et
als. (The names are hard to read and don't seem to pertain to the
Lower Norfolk County area)

17 Apr 1669 - MAJR: WM: BALL & MR. THOMAS CHETWOOD 1600 acres in Rap-
   (p68)   pahannock County for trans: of 32 persons: JOSEPH FOSTER,
                WILL: HAGGARD, EDWARD SALTER, et als.

9 Oct 1667 - EDMUND HUGGARTE et als headrights in patent to COLL:
   (p78)   EDMOND SCARBURGH in Accomac County.

31 Dec 1667 - RICHARD AYLIFFE - This is a patent to ABRAHAM FLOOD and
   (p92)   RICH: CARTER 150 acres on Stafford County. ROBERT HOUSE-
                ING sold land unto RICHARD AYLIFFE and he sold to ABRAHAM
FLOOD & RICHARD CARTER as by bill of sale recorded in Stafford County
dated 18 Apr 1666.

31 Dec 1667 - MR. ROBT: KING & ANTHONY HOGGARD 737 acres in Stafford
   (p93)   County ....trans: of JOHN BENNETT, JOHN MARSHALLM ROBERT
                WHITEHEAD.....et als........(very faded.

9 Dec 1667 - LANCASTER LOVETT 700 acres in Lower Norfolk County in
   (p105)   Lynhaven Parish butting Easterly upon a former divident
                of land belonging to the sd. Lovett commonly called the
"Labor in Vayne" Ely upon the land of RENATUS LAND and the lands of JNO:
MARTIN Sly upon the land of ffRANCIS LAND commonly called "POULTRYES HALL"

500 acres thereof being formerly granted to the sd. Lovett by Patent
dated 20 Oct 1661 and 200 acres the residue being newly taken up and
due by and for the trans: of 4 persons: RICH: HARRELL, THO: STANBRIDGE,
ELIZABETH TRANT (or GRANT), ELIZABETH THORNEDON.

29 Jan 1667 - ROBT: THURSTON and PETER THURSTON transported to Parish
   (p105)   Chuckatuck by MILES & RICHARD LEWIS.

4 Apr 1667 - JNO: MANING transported to RAPPA: County by THOS: GOLD-
   (p105)   MAN.

30 Aug 1665 - THOS: NORCOTT 472 acres in Western Branch of Elizabeth
   (p110)   River Begin: at a small gutt & soe runing 160 po joyne-
               ing to the land of JAMES HARRIS and soe NW 220 po to a
mkd oake & soe SW 60 po to a mked oake butting on the land of THOMAS
WRIGHT & soe W joyneing to Wrights land 140 po to a mkd oake & soe N
180 po to a mkd tree & soe W 200 po to a mkd tree & S 180 po butting
on the land of RICHARD STARNELL & soe E 200 po to a mkd oake & soe
S 40 po to a mkd red oake &c.................. ....
due , 200 acres formerly granted JNO: DEWARE by patent 20 Mar 1653 &
by him assigned to sd. NORCOTT. Residue for trans of -blank - .

1 Dec 1666 - Land of JOHN WATKINS & MR. THOMAS WOODHOUSE adjacent the
   (p112)   the GLEBE LAND of SOUTHWARKE PARISH in Surry Co.

13 Mar 1667/8 - RICHARD YEATES 450 acres in Southern Branch of Eliz-
   (p112)   beth River being a parcell of land lying between the
               lands of FRANCIS SAWYER (SAYER) and his owne land beg:
at a marked Gum & soe running NE 75 po to a mkd oake and soe NW 320 po
butting the land of ffRANCIS SAWYER to a mkd pine by the branch side
and soe up by the branch side SW 75 po to a mkd pine butting on his
own land & soe SE 320 po joyneing to his own land to the first station
Sd. land being due unto YEATES (viz) 300 acs part hereof formerly
granted unto CAPT. THO: WILLOUGHBY by patent dated 28 Feb 1636 and by
sd. WILLOUGHBY assigned unto JOHN YEATES & due RICH: as heire of afsd.
JNO: & 150 acres the residue for trans. of 3 persons Rights out of a
Relinquister (sic) pattent bearsing date 4 May 1636 granted to RICH:
YEATES the Elder. (the only patent to Tho. Willoughby in 1636 is the
patent dated 13 Feb 1636 which is the land in Norfolk Borough. Nugent
p 54 which land is not on the Southern Branch but on the Eastern
Branch, the North side of. AGW)

16 Mar 1667/8 - JOHN SEXTON 1000 acres in New Kent County for trans.
   (p114)   of NICH: POOLE, WM: IVEY, JAMES WILSON et als..........

19 Apr 1668 - PETER SMITH 400 acres in Lower Norfolk County being in
   (p120)   a branch of the Western Branch of Elizabeth River. 200
               acres part thereof bounding beg: at the East side of
LOYDS CREEK at a mkd hiccory standing by EDMOND BOWMANS mkd trees and
running for breadth along the creek side ENE 100 po to a Red Oake
standing at a point at the mouth of a branch called Reedy branch along
the branch side SSE into the wood 320 po to a mkd red oake & thence

WSW into the Swampe & through the Swampe to MR. BOWMANS mkd trees & soe
down by sd trees 320 po to the first station & 200 acres the residue
beginning at a mkd pine standing on a point by the Creeke side & soe
running ENE 100 po downe by the Creeke side to a mkd pine standing by
the Creek side & soe to a mkd oake butting on his own land and soe
NNW 320 po joyning to his owne land to the first station 200 acres of
sd land being formerly granted unto sd PETER SMITH by pattent dated
9 Dec 1665 & 200 acres being due for trans: of 4 persons: HENRY HARPER,
THO: DINNING, THO: BEALE, JOHN MARSTON.

29 Apr 1668 - THOMAS BATTS & HENRY BATTS sones of MR. JNO: BATTS decd.
   (p126)   5800 acres South side of JAMES RIVER in Chas. City County
                for trans: of 118 persons: JNO: ADAMS, JNO: BATTE SR &
JR., WM: BATTE, THO: BATTE, HEN: BATTE, RICH: POOLE, et als (all the
names are given) (Note: Batts in patent - Batte in head right list)

26 Apr 1668 - MR. RICH: CHURCH 550 acres in Lower Norfolk County on
   (p148)   the S side of the Eastern Branch of Elizabeth River beg:
               at a mkd pyne standing on a Poynt on the East side of a
creeke called BILLINGSGALE CREEK & soe bounded on the Creeke into the
woods all poynts included Sw & by S 320 po & bounding on the corner tree
of WILLIAM JOYCE & from thence E 73 po to a mkd white oak bounding on
RICH: WHITBYS lyne & soe E 150 po to a mkd pine standing on a poynt in
a creeke called NEHUNTREES CREEK & soe runnign down the creek NE 160 po
to the mouth of the creek 240 po to a mkd pine & th: W along the river
side 125 po to the first station. 500 acres of this land being purchased of TYMOTHY IVES by bill of sale recorded in Lower Norfolk County
(date not given) & 50 acres for transportation of one person: ROBERT
TIRRELL.

26 7ber 1669 - GILES COLES 120 acres in WARWICK COUNTY at a Beaver dam
   (p153)   &c...Wly upon land of ROBERT GILLETT sd land being due sd.
               COLES by Inheritance from THO: STEPHENS which land was due
to the sd. STEPHENS by pattent dated 5 Mar 1652 and now renewed in sd.
COLES name........

17 Mar 1667 - WM: CARNEY 100 acres in the Western Branch of Elizabeth
   (p167)   River........begin: at a marked pine by CLARKES CREEK and
               soe for length NNE 320 po to a mkd gum and soe for bredth
NNW 50 po into a pond and soe again for length SSW 320 po to a mkd pine
standing by the Creek side and soe again for bredth ESE 50 po down by
the Creek side to the first station. sd. land formerly granted to RICH:
STARNELL by pattent dated 11 Jan 1652 & sd STARNELL dying by his last
will & Testament gave & bequeathed the same to the sd. RICHARD CARNEY.
(no explanation of why William Carney received the patent, probably a
son of Richard.) Note: RICHARD STARNELL 11 Jan 1652 - Patent 100 acres
on Western Branch of Eliz. Riv. beg. at CLERKES CREEK & running for
length NNE &c for trans. of two persons WILLIAM RAMPSIE, SAMUEL QUILT.
by assignment from MR. RO: HUBBERD. Nugent 269 (AGW) Same land as above.

27 Apr 1667 - CAPT: LAWRENCE BAKER 2050 acres in Surry County. The
   (167)   headrights include: CAPT: LAWR: BAKER twice, ELIZA: his

wife, JNO: his son, JAMES his son, JANE, RICH: & ANNE REEVE, ALICE LEE,
JANE DOWNER, ANNE MILLINGTON, JNO: MACOM (MARKHAM?), JAMES WILSON, ROBT:
BRUCE, JOHN SLOOPE? et als...........

26 Apr 1670 - MORRIS ffEGARRELL (FITZGERALD?) 200 acres in Lower Norfolk
   (p194)   in right of his wife KATHERINE who was the relict of ROBER
               HOWARD decd....according to the ancient bounds thereof &
lately -(faded)- to escheat &c........and is now granted to ye sd. MOR-
RIS ffEGARRELL in ye right of afsd............&c.......................
(The name is written thusly:

7 Dec 1668 - THOMAS HARWARR (also THO: HARWARE in same record) & NICH:
   (p205)   COX 900 acres in Rappahannock Co.

8 Feb 1668/9 - MIHILL GOWREE (MICK GOWREE in same record, probably
   (p208)   meant to be Michaell?) 30 or 40 acres in Merchants Hundred
               Parrish in James City County formerly belonging to JOHN
TURNER decd. and by him purchased of CAPT. RICHARD BARNEHOUSE and lately
found to escheat to his Maties &c.......rec. in the Sect. Office under
the hand & seales of COLL MILES CAREY ESQ for the sd County sworne before him 20 Dec 1666....now granted the said MICK GOWREE..............
(The names
         Turner   Mick   )

         MIHILL -

1 Mar 1668/9 - STEPHEN DURDEN   250 acres in upper parrish of the county
   (p209)   of Nansemond.....near land of ROBERT HOOKES (or STOOKES)
               and ISRAEL JOHNSON....for trans: of 5 persons: JOHN
THUMER? (written thusly: et als................

14 May 1669 - MR. THO: IKEN   1350 acres in right of his wife ELIZABETH
   (218)   late wife of MR. EDWARD GRIFFITH decd. lying in MULBERRY
               ISLAND parrish in WARWICK COUNTY &c.......on a point at
the mouth of a creeke nere the now dwelling house of sd THO: IKEN....
BAKERS NECK where the Church formerly stood ......runing along the bank
of JAMES RIVER unto the old point....by the waterside and the Great
Marsh which divideth this land from MULBARY ISLAND.......GEORGE HARWOODS
line & bounded on these two dist?xxxx by the land of JOHN BASSE.........
Cart path......HARWOODS & BREWERS line of trees &c.....................
POWLES land on the side of Bedlam? Marsh .....CAULLEYS lyne....E by N to
a mkd white oake on WARWICK RIVER.......neare mouth of BUTLERS BRIDGE
CREEK......up the N br. of that Creek which branch divideth this land &
that of CAPT: THO: ffLYNT.....to head of BUTLERS CREEK swamp.......being
part of a dividt: conteyning 1150 acres being granted to divers other
persons as per records of WARWICK COUNTY COURT may appeare 400 acres of
overplus is found herein and is due P: trans: of 8 persons: WM: WHARTON,
THEO: POTTER, RICH ffOXHALL, WM: WHITAKER, HENRY MORGAN, MARY LORD, THO:
NEEDLEY, THOMAS a negro.

20 Jul 1669 - JOHN HERBERT 1227 acres in Lower Norfolk County upon W
    (p220)   side of Southern Branch of Elizabeth River beg: at a mkd
                pine standing upon a point & soe running SSW 396 po by
the MAINE RIVER side to the mouth of a creeke called DEEP CREEKE thence
WNW 496 po up the sd Creeke to a small creeke called GOOS(E the e is off
the edge of the page) to a marked pine thence NNE 396 po to the land of
JOHN MANNING soe ESE 496 po by DUELING (   ) CREEKE & the River
side to the Sd. JOHN HERBERT by patent (   ) dated 1 Oct 1662 &
350 acres other part thereof by pattent datted 11 Mar 1664 and 527 acs.
the residue for trans: of 11 persons: JNO:
ELIZABETH BANKES, JNO: a Scott, GEO: (Horwod?),
GREEN, MARY GOODRICH, SUSAN POOLE, WM:
GREEN, JNO: WALLER, JNO: CLARK, MARY JONE, JAMES HARLOW.

14 Sep 1667 - JOHN MANNING 300 acres on the East side of the SOUTHERNE
    (p220)   BRANCH of ELIZABETH RIVER in Lower Norfolk County begin:
at a hiccory standing by the side of a creek called HATTONS? CREEKE &
soe running 32 po W by the side of sd Creeke to a pine standing on a
point upon the MAINE RIVER thence N 210 po downe the riverside to a
pine & soe E by S 320 po into the woods & from thence 90 po adjoyning
to sd MANNINGS lands to the first station....200 acres formerly granted
to sd. MANNING by pat dated 25 Oct 1648 and 100 acres the residue for
trans: of 2 persons: JOHN CARPENTER & LUKE WHITE. (Note: The Hattons
Creeke above is faded and I believe it is GATHERS CREEKE see what follows AGW) In Nugent p 180 - 25 Oct 1648 JOHN MANNING 200 acres Low.
Norf. Co. Upon Northward side of GAYTHERS CREEK being a branch of the
Southward Branch of Eliz. Riv. runing unto land of MERMADICKE MERRING-
TON ...&c........

14 Sep 1667 - WM: CHICHESTER 220 acres on the North side of DAN'L: TAN-
    (p220)   NERS CREEKE in Lower Norfolk County begin: at a pine stand-
                ing on a small point of a Creeke from thence NE 160 po to
a small Creeke & from thence 160 po SW to the first station due for trans:
of 5 persons: JAMES GARLAND, TYMOTHY RICE, MARY RINGLY, MARK TOMLYN,
JOHN SEABORNE.

14 Sep 1667 - HENRY HOLSTEAD (HALSTEAD?) 58 acres on the SOUTH SIDE of
    (221)   the EASTERN BRANCH of ELIZA: RIV. at the head of the
                JULIAN CREEK joyning to the W side of his owne land in
Lower Norfolk County begin: at a red oake & running 40 po W to the lyne
of THOMAS RICHARDSONS land & from thence SSW 160 po to a pine standing
by the side of a branch & from thence 60 po E bownding on WM: WHITEHURST
land & soe NNE 160 po to the first station sd. land due for trans: of
one person: ELIZ: BRIGHT.

14 Sep 1667 - RICHARD NICHOLLS 320 acres of land on the SOUTH SIDE of
    (p221)   the EASTERNE BRANCH of ELIZ: RIV. in Lower Norfolk County
                begin: at a red oake joyneing on the South side of 120
acres of his owne land & running 260 po S by W to a gum adjoyneing to
the E side of MOSES LYNTONS land and from th: 130 po Ely xxxxxx to a
white oake and soe 260 po N by E along by ADAM DOTTARDS (or Dollards?)
mkd trees to a red oake and soe 130 po W to the first station. 120 acres

part thereof being part of a pettent of 250 acres granted to ROBERT
MARTYN beareing date the 12 Oct 1638 & by sd MARTYN sold to THOS: MILES
& by sd MILES sold to NICHOLLS as by bill of sale dated 4 Jun 1645 and
the assgmt: to NICHOLLS from MILES dated 8 Sep 1649 & 200 acres the
residue for trans: of 4 psons: THO: EASTFIELD, PETER MARTYN, ROWLD:
MARKE, OWEN HOLLAND.

14 Sep 1667 - JOHN *Slow* (Slow or should this be Stow?) 640 acres on
   (221)   the WEST SIDE of the SOUTHERN BRANCH of ELIZA: RIV. on the
               N side of a Creeke called DEEP CREEKE in Lower Norfolk Co.
begin: at a hiccory his fathers corner tree amd running NNW 320 po up
the branch side and from thence ENE 320 po into the woods and from thence
SSE 320 po joyneing to his fathers land and from thence WSW 320 po to
the first station.....for trans: of 13 psons: JAMES ENDFIELD, MATTHEW
FIRTH, ROBT: DALLISON, JEREMY NEEVE, TYMOTHY WARE, ROWLAND MEERES, JNO:
WHITE, JAMES ALLINGTON, ARTHUR HICKMAN, MARY HART, WM: HAYNES, JACOB
DeHAY, BRUCE MATROM.

14 Sep 1667 - THOMAS ffENFORD 50 acres on the WEST SIDE of the SOUTHERN
   (p222)   BRANCH of ELIZ: RIV. in Lower Norfolk County begin: at a
corner tree of his owne land and runing NE by N 80 po to a pine standing
in the Marsh and from thence NW 160 po by the river side th: 80 po
SW by S and from th: 100 po SE by S joyneing his owne land to the first
station due for trans: of one person: RICHARD MORRIS.

14 Sep 1667 - THOM: HARRIS 97 acres on the NORTH SIDE of DANL: TANNERS
   (p222)   CREEKE in the County of Lower Norfolk begin: at a white
               oak running 140 po SW up a small branch to a white oak
standing by the branch side thence 40 po NW bounding upon MR. THO: FUL-
CHERS to a gum and from thence 130 po NE to a red oak and soe 120 po
SE to the first station. For trans: of 4 persons: WM: MOSSE, ROBT:
TAUNTON, PETER ABRAMS, HEN: LOUND? *Lound*

14 Sep 1667 - NICHOLAS WILLIAMS 200 acres on the NORTH SIDE of DANL:
   (p222)   TANNERS CREEK in Lower Norfolk Co. begin: at a pine stand-
               ing on a point by the branch side & running 100 po SE by E
upon the Maine Creek to a pine standing by the side of a small branch
& soe 320 po NE by N to a red oake & from thence 100 po NW by W thence
SW by S 320 po to the first station. For trans: of 4 persons: HERBERT
EMMETT, GEORGE JONES, HANNA EMMERSON, ROGER THORLY.

14 Sep 1667 - JOHN CORPOREW (CORPREW?) 200 acres on SOUTH SIDE of EAST-
   (p222)   ERN BRANCH of the INDIAN CREEK in Elizabeth River in Low-
               er Norfolk Co. beginning at a red oake & running S into
the woods joyning to WM: MORRYS (MURRAY or MORRIS?) 320 po thence 30 po
 W to WM: WHITEHEADS corner tree & from thence 320 po N by the branch
side to a small branch adjoyning to MOSES LINTON thence E 170 po to the
first station. For transportation of 4 persons: (Names not given)

12 May 1669 - GEO: MOORE 1400 acres in ISLE OF WIGHT COUNTY. Head
   (p222)   rights: JNO: HEABERD (or HERBERT?) *Hinkson* (Herbers?)

ROBT: BENNETT, THO: ELWES, WM: POWELL, RICH: BENNETT, ROBT: SCOTT et als.

10 Aug 1669 - THOS: BRIDGE(s?) 750 acres in Lower Norfolk County in
   (p234)   LYNNHAVEN PARRISH begin at a mkd oake stump running SE
                 by S 300 po along by LT: COLL: LAMBERTS markt trees to
a markt white oake in the swamp thence WSW 300 po to a markt white oak by
the side of a swamp thence W by N 300 po to a markt pine thence N by W
320 po to a markt oake by a path which leadeth from MR. HOSKINS to MR.
THO: BRIDGES thence ENE 200 po to a markt pokecory? standing by the
head of a branch thence along sd. branch S by W 200 po to the first
station. 256 acres of sd. land due by former pattent to MR. BRIDGE(S?)
dated 25 Mar 1655 & 150 acres by the sd BRIDGE purchased from HENRY
SNAILE and 344 acres the residue for transportation of 7 persons: JAMES
TOOLTON, SARAH EDICK, RICHARD WILLIAMS & WIFE, ROBERT SPEED, ANN BEALE.

22 Apr 1669 - ROBERT TUCKER 100 acres in WESTERN BRANCH of ELIZ: RIV:
   (p242)   begin: at a mkd Spanish Oake & soe running SW 320 po
                 joyning to ye land of the widd: JENNINGS to a mkd white
oake NW 50 po to a mkd gum soe NE 320 po to a mkd stake and joyneing to
the land of JNO: ELLOTT soe SE 50 po to the first station & for trans:
of 2 persons: RICH: MURFFEE (MURPHY?) & NATH: DEBBLE (or DIBBLE) (Note:
John Ellott in this patent may be Elliott or Ellett. The name Ellett
in Norfolk County Records is and was Elliot depending upon the way the
clerk spelled it)(AGW)

24 Jul 1669 - JAMES WALLACE 990 acres in Charles City County formerly
   (p248)   granted to THO: WHEELER and found to escheat ....
                 now granted to JAMES WALLACE. (no head rights)

15 Oct 1659 - THO: GOODRICH 1800 acres in Rappahannock County........
   (p254)   due for trans: of 36 persons: RICE (or RICH:) ?AGGETT
                 (the first letter of this name is almost obliterated, it
                 could be either H or P - Haggett or Paggett?),RICE JONES,
JNO: JAMES, RICH TURNER , JNO: DAVYES, THO: BARRINGTON, et als........

24 Oct 1669 - *Borton* & JNO: THERMAN (or SHERMAN) *Jno Thorman*
   (p254)   WM: PORTEN, WM: LANGLEY head rights in patent to LT. COLL:
                 THOS: GOODRICH 2876 acres in Rappahannock County.

29 Oct 1669 - RICHARD HEABEARD (RICHARD HABEART in margin) 1539 acres
   (p257)   in Stafford County.....near the land of JNO: & WM: HEA-
                 BEARD......twenty persons. (names are given)

30 Oct 1669 - THOMAS STOE 640 acres in Lower Norfolk County in ELIZA:
   (p271)   RIV: upon the N side of DEEPE CREEK beg: upon a point at
                 a mkd tree of JNO: (CEVREG ?)*Cevreg* thence runn-
ing NW 320 po by the run side to a marked pokberry thence NE 320 po to
a mkd oake SE 320 po to a mkd pine thence SW 320 po to the first station
for trans: of 13 persons: THO: SENIOR, ELIZ: SENIOR, JNO: STOE, THO:
STOE, ROBT: JACOB, GEO: ROOKINS, MARY DUELIN (Doolin?), ISACK, ANN, SUSAN,
ELIZ: STOW. (Note: The name of Etheridge has been spelled many ways in
the Norfolk Co. Records, Eavrge, Everg, &c. they lived in Deep Creek) AGW

29 Oct 1669 - DAVID MURRAY 600 acres on the SOUTH SIDE of the EASTERN
   (p275)   BRANCH of ELIZ: RIVER in Lower Norfolk County begin: at
               a mkd red oake & running W 320 po to a mkd red oake th:
S 300 po joyneing to the land of WM: WHITEHOUSE and so running away E
320 po to a mkd pine th: N 300 po to the first station. 400 acres of
sd 600 acres belonging to him sd. DAVID MURRAY by a former pattent and
200 acres for transportation of 4 persons: JNO: KNOWLE, JNO: BROWNE,
MARY PAGE (of GAGE), THO: WEBSTER.

5 Jul 1669 - JOHN SANDERS 650 acres in Warwick County and MULBERRY
   (p282)   ISLAND PARRISH and on a Creeke called SCKIFFES CREEKE
               ....land of CAPT: ROBERT PYLAND. 500 acres formerly
granted by SIR JOHN HARVEY to JACOB AVERY for 21 year lease dated 2 Feb
1630/1 which land afterwards granted to WM: RAVENETT by 3 severall pattents: one for 150 acres dated 21 Nov 1635, the second 250 acres 23
Sep 1636, the third 100 acres 20 Feb 1638/9 and by RAVENETT given to
his daughter SUSANNA now wife of sd JOHN SANDERS by his last will &
testament dated 20 Mar 1656 and the residue 150 acres for trans: of
3 persons: THO: DOWIN, EDW: HOARD, CISLEY JORDEN.

22 Apr 1670 - WARWICK CAMMOCK 1923 acres in Rappahhannock County for
   (p286a)   trans: of 39 psons: JOSEPH CORNICH (CORNISH?) 6 tymes,
               JNO: & WM: BLAKE each 6 tymes, .THO: SHEPPARD 6 tymes,
MARY FLETCHER, GEO: HOLLIS, FRA: GITMAN? *gitman* EDWARD SWIFT,
THO: PALMER, DAVID HOLT, GEO: HAYNES,   RICH: WORKHAM,
WM: DYER, MARY DYER, ALIX: HOBBS, JANE DENNES, EMANUEL TALBOTT & his
wife REBECCA his daughter. (the way this last is written Rebecca
could be both wife and daughter or wife , or daughter. ?? AGW)

30 Jul 1670 - WILLIAM PEBLES 473 acres in Charles City County, Head
   (p289)   rights include: FFRA: HOWGOOD, GILES WRIGHT, WM: LANGLAND
et als.   *Hawgood*

17 Jun 1670 - JAMES TURNER 786 acres in New Kent County..............
   (p290)   (bounds and head rights are given)

18 Apr 1670 - MR. WM: MOSELEY 427 acres in Rappahannock County sd land
   (p296)   being due for trans: of 9 persons: JOHN PAGE, HEN: BAR-
               LOE, ROG: TYNE, WM: SHORT, ANN JACKSON, TYM: JAMES, THO:
PRATT, RICH: ALBARNE or ALBANE.

30 Oct 1669 - HENRY NICHOLAS 300 acres on the SOUTH SIDE of the EASTERN
   (p297)   BRANCH of ELIZ: RIV: beg: at a mkd white oake thence S
               into the woods 320 po to a mkd red oake thence W by N 240
po to a mkd spanish oake standing in a branch by a runn and soe running
nigh the said runn 320 po to a mkd gum standing in the sd Runn thence
E by S 140 po to the first station 100 acs part thereof formerly granted
22 Nov 1651 the residue being due for the trans: of 4 psons: JOHN
WRIGHT, MARY LAWRENCE, JNO: LEGGETT, ROB: LUELLNS (Lewellyn?).

18 Apr 1670 - HUMPHREY HARWOOD   1644 acres on the North Side of SKEATHS
   (p304)   CREEK in Warwick County........OWEN MORRIS his land......
               land of CAPT: NATH: HURD..........land being formerly
granted to CAPT: THOS: HARWOOD by pattent dated 26 Nov 1652............
overplus of land.......trans of 12 psons: JOHN BERROW, ROB PERRY, WILL:
LAMBEMETT, JOHN WEBSTER, ANN BURGESS, THO: SCOTT, RICH: SMITH, THO:
HUDSON, BAPTIST STARR, THO: SEQUIER, HENRY STOCKMAN, THO: SCOTCH.

30 Sep 1670 - MR. GEORGE DURANT   700 acres in Lower Norfolk County on E
   (p306)   side of ye NORTH RIVER which falleth into COROTOKE (Curri-
               tuck) begin: at a mkd redd oake standing by a small Creek
side issuing out of the sd. river which divideth this land from the
land of MR: THOMAS TULIES (or JULIES) (Note: this name could be Ivlies)
& soe running N to ye sd River 350 po to another mkd redd oake standing
by another branch side issuing out of ye sd river which branch divideth
this land from ye land called MASSOPUNGO thence E by a line of mkd trees
320 po into ye woods & from thence S 350 po & thence W 320 po to ye first
station....for trans: of 14 pers: THO: BRUSH, ROBT: BRUSH, HEN: MACRA,
RICH: WILLIS, PETER BELSON, JNO: ffOX, ROBERT WILKINSON, ANNE DOUSE
RICH: READ, HENRY TOWNSEND, HEN: THUCKER, ROBT: DUCEING, PETER ROBIN-
SON, JEFFREY SNEAD.

30 Sep 1670 - PATRICKE WHITE   160 acres in Lower Norfolk County on the
   (p308)   WEST SIDE of the NORTH RIVER which falleth into COROTOKE
               beginning at a mkd pine tree which standeth in a small
branch that falleth into ye sd River & soe runeth S downe by ye side of
a GREAT MARSH that faceth ye River 80 po to a mkd white oake that standeth in another branch which falleth into ye sd river and thence W by a
line of mkd trees 320 po into ye woods, thence N 80 po and y^t E 320 po
to ye first station &c....due for trans: of 3 persons: JNO: MORSE,
REBECCA HORNEFIELD, SAMPSON KIRBY.

7 Oct 1670 - WILLIAM MOSELEY & NICHOLAS CATTLET   646 acres in Rappahan-
   (p320)   nock County. (head rights are given)

10 Oct 1670 - LANCASTER LOVETT   1200 acres in parish of LYNHAVEN in
   (p321)   Lower Norfolk County on the SOUTH SIDE of a branch of
               BENNETTS CREEK parting this land from the land of JOHN
MARTIN decd and on the Southeastern side of another branch of BENNETTS
CREEK parting this land from the lands of THOMAS GOODACRE, WILLIAM
GOODACRE, THOMAS DAVIS, BENONY BURROWS and the land of MAJOR ADAM THO-
ROWGOOD called TIMBER NECKE beginning at a peninsula comonly called by
the name of a LITTLE ISLAND where BENETS CREEKE divides itself into
three branches and from thence running SWward upon one of the Branches
side to a poynt where the Creeke er branch turneth Southward and then
by the Northeastern side thereof a line of mkd trees Drawn from the
branch SE by E which parteth this land from the land of RICHARD POOLE
allsoe runing from the aforesaid peninsula Eastward up the other branch
of BENETS CREEK unto a line of mkd trees drawne from the N side thereof
E by N 194 po unto the mkd trees of the land patterned by RENATUS LAND
and along the sd lands mkd trees first SW 348 po unto the Corner mkd
tree of the sd LAND his land and then SE 224 po to another corner tree

of the said LAND his land and from thence by a right line unto the land
of RICHARD POOLE decd then along the head of the sd POOLE his land NE
by N unto the afsd: SE by E line. 700 acres pte: thereof being formerly granted sd LOVETT by Patt: dated 9 Dec 1667. The other 500 being
newly taken up and due for trans of 10 psons: ROBERT GLASCOCK, DEBORAH
GLASCOCK, ELIZABETH BRAY, ROBERT BIRD, ffRANCIS BRIGHT, THOMAS SHEPARD,
WILLIAM XXLMAN *ffman* (COLMAN?), JOHN BIGG, JOHN WILKINSON, MATHEW
READ.

10 Oct 1670 - LANCASTER LOVETT 300 acres in Lower Norfolk County begin:
   (p322)   at the SANDY BANKES by LINCOLNE (Linkhorn Bay AGW) at a
              mkd gum thence running W by a line of mkd trees seperating
this land from the land now in the possession of PLUMER BRAY and bounded on the Southeastern parts therby 150 po thence N 320 po into the
DESERT and bounded Wwardly upon the GREATE FRESH POND soe E 150 po to
the BANCKES of the MAINE OCEAN (the Sand Dunes?) soe S 320 po to the
place where it began due for trans: of 6 psons: RICHARD ffARMER
THOMAS STANTON, JOHN ABRELL, NICHOLAS WILLIS, JOHN GIBSON MATHEW DANETT.

10 Oct 1670 - COLL: THOMAS DEW 750 acres in Upper Northfolke on ye
   (p323)   EASTERN SIDE of ye SOUTHERN BRANCH of NANZIMOND RIVER &c
              ....formerly granted 8 Jan 1643. (see Nugent 151)

26 Apr 1670 - SAMUEL GRANBURY 125 acres in NANSEMOND COUNTY according
   (p333)   to the ancient &c...........formerly granted to RALPH
              BROADHURST decd and later found to escheat to his Maties
&c.......................

20 Oct 1670 - ARTHUR MOSELEY 550 acres in LYNHAVEN PARRISH in Lower
   (p334)   Norfolk County begin: at a mkd pine at the point by the
              riverside & soe running SE by E 270 po to a mkd pine at
the head of a branch and soe N by E 320 po to a mkd pine thence NW by W
270 po to a great mkd pine by the side of a branch out of the BROAD
CREEK thence S by W 300 po to the first Station. The sd land being formerly granted to MR. WILLM: MOSELEY father of the said ARTH: MOSELEY
by patt: dated 17 Feb 1652 and by the sd WM: MOSELEY by his last will
& testament given and bequeathed unto the sd ARTHUR MOSELEY &c........
(see 1652 pat to William Moseley in Nugent p 275)

21 Oct 1670 - CAPT: JOHN WEST 200 acres in Accomac County betweene
   (p335)   ANDIN? and COROTOCKE CREEKES....bounded on the South by
              land of RICHARD JOHNSON & WILLIAM WALTER.................
(This one is hard to read, some words faded out. AGW)

19 Oct 1670 - HENRY & ELIZABETH LAWRENCE 350 acres in NORTHWEST BRANCH
   (p337)   of NANSEMOND RIVER ....butting on the land of ROB-
              ERT LAWRENCE.....250 acres of this land formerly granted
to HUMPHREY EDEY by patt dated 27 Dec 1652 and 100 acres being purchased
by the sd EDEY of JNO: LOYD as by conveyance dated 25 Mar 1652..........
both which parcells were given by the will of the sd EDEY to the sd
HENRY & ELIZABETH.   (see Nugent p 236)

25 Nov 1670 - JNO: CHADWELL   650 acres in Lower Norfolk County begin:
   (344)   at a Marked Beech tree standing on the Eastermost side
                of a Swamp called RIDGEFORD SWAMP being a branch of ELIZ-
BETH RIVER and running thence E 320 po to a mkd gum & thence N by E
325 po to a mkd oake thence W 320 po to another mkd beech standing alsoe
on the side of RIDGEFORD SWAMP and soe up sd branch to the first mentioned mkd tree &c.........trans: of 13 psons: WM: THOMAS, MATH: WILLIAMS,
JNO: SHORT, ALEX: DAVIS, CHA: GREEN, JNO: RIPPON, WM: SANDS, EDWD:
ffROST, WM: JONES, THO: CARR, EDW: COOPER, ffRA: BARBER, xxxx BALL.

PATENT BOOK 6 PART I ends with p 350 - PART II begins with p 351.

7 Apr 1671 - GEORGE POOLE, RICHARD FARTHINGALE & RICH: BARMINGHAM &
   (p352)   JAMES ffORSITH   800 acres in Gloster County in WARE PARR-
                ISH formerly granted to HENRY CORBELL By patt dated 6 Mar
1653/4 & by him assigned to the sd POOLE, ffARTHINGALE, BARMINGHAM &
ffORSET. The head rights names are faded.

3 Apr 1670 - HENRY WOODHOUSE   740 acres in LYNHAVEN in the County of
   (p357)   Lower Norfolk... 500 acres thereof beginning at the mouth
of the LITTLE BAY and runing along the West side of the Bay S 282 po to
a mkd white oake from thence W 182 (or 282) po to a mkd pohicory and
soe N 302 po to a mkd red oake from thence E 282 po to the first station.
        200 acres thereof begin: at a mkd white oake Joyneing to the above
500 acres and runing S by the bay side 100 po to a mkd red oake thence
320 po W into the woods thence N 100 po and soe away E joyning to the
afsd 500 acres 320 po to the first station.
        25 acres beginning at the NW side of the afsd land runing N 100 po
bounding upon JNO: WOODHOUSE & thence E 4 po by the bay side and from
there S 100 po joyneing upon the said former land and soe away W 40 po
to the first station.
        & 15 acres joyneing to the E side of the aforesaid land lying
NW and SE in a Neck by the Bay side.
        500 acres whereof being formerly granted to MR. HEN: WOODHOUSE by
patt dated 22 May 1637 & 200 acres part of a patt granted to JOHN MOY
the 5 May 1638 & by purchase came to sd HEN: WOODHOUSE and 45 acres by
& for trans: of one person: THOMAS CREED.
        (The 500 acre patent - 22 May 1637 - "within the mouth of the
second baye from the LONG CREEK of the Ewd side of CHISOPEIAKE RIV.
(Lynnhaven River) N & S along the baye, E uponthe baye & W into the
woods.........." This Henry Woodhouse was deceased by 1670 and is
the father of the above Henry Woodhouse. AGW) (see Nugent p 57)

24 May 1671 - WILLM: ROGERS   100 acres on the S side of the EASTERN BR:
   (p361)   of the ELIZ: RIVER begin: at a mkd white oake standing by
                a run & bounding on JAMES WHITEHURST miles end & running
WNW 100 po to a mkd gum & th: SSW 160 po to a mkd white oake & th: ESE
100 po to a mkd Pine standing in a Branch & soe NNE by or nigh the
branch side to the first mentioned station due for the transportation
of 2 persons: JNO: THOMSON, WM: HIX?

25 Jul 1672 - THO: RICHARDSON 50 acres in Lower Norfolk County begin:
  (363)   at a mkd red oake by the side of DEEP NECK near the mouth
               of GOOSE CREEKE & running NW $\frac{1}{2}$ Nly by the said GOOSE CR:
butting on another parcell of land of the sd RICHARDSON 152 po to a mkd
pine in a swamp neare the head of the same creeke thence SW $\frac{1}{2}$ Wly 52 po
butting on the land of JOHN CHERRY to a mkd Gum by a pocoson thence
SE $\frac{1}{2}$ Sly to a pine by the side of DEEP CREEKE 152 (po?) thence to the
first mentioned mkd tree. for trans: of one person: THO: PRESCOATE.

6 Aug 1671 - CAPT: WM: CORKER 1850 acres in Surry County. Among the
  (p366)   37 headrights: JOHN THURMAN (or JOHN STURMAN) written
               (Could this be JOHN THURMER?)

6 Apr 1671 - GEORGE WEBB 50 acres in Elizabeth City County formerly
  (p370)   granted to DAVID POOLE and lately found to escheat......
               now granted to sd GEORGE WEBB.

6 Apr 1671 - JONE POOLE (could be Jane?) 474 acres in Elizabeth City
  (p370)   County, sd land formerly granted to JNO: POOLE decd. and
               later found to escheat......now granted to JONE POOLE.

6 Apr 1671 - WILLIAM MORRIS 150 acres in Elizabeth City County for-
  (p370)   merly granted to DAVID POOLE decd and lately found to
               escheat.........now granted to sd WILLIAM MORRIS.

9 Feb 1670/1- EDWARD HOLLYER 200 acres in Lower Norfolk County in Lyn-
  (p371)   haven Parish at the head of Lynhaven River beginning at a
               young marked Cipres (Cypress) standing on the Northerne
side of a run and on the Western side the head of Lynhaven River neare
a place called the HOLLOW POPLAR and running from the said Cipres E 74
po & thence N 100 po thence W 320 po thence S 100 po thence E 246 po being newly taken up as abovesaid the said land being due for transportation of 4 persons: ROBERT ROSSE, MARY MYNNS, PETER RANS (or RAUS) HEN:
CLAY.

3 8ber 1671 - WILLM: BROCK 350 acres in Lower Norfolk County in Lynn-
  (p375)   haven Parrish at the head of the FRESH POND in DAM NECK
               and bounded on the Northerne parts by the said pond and
the Westerne pt (part) by the Dams & its pocosons or swamp...........
begin: at a mkd tree at the Southside of the FRESH POND and thence runing S 220 po thence SW by W$\frac{1}{2}$ point Wly 336 po thence NW by W -faded- Nly
48 po into a pocoson of the Dams then downe the side of sd Pocoson and
Dams unto the first beginning for transportation of 7 persons: MORRIS
ffEGARELL (Fitzgerald?), JAMES -faded- , RICH: WELCH, MARY -faded-, (the
rest of the names are impossible to read they are so faded)

3 Oct 1671 - EDMOND MOORE 400 acres in Lower Norfolk County in Lynn-
  (p375)   haven Parish begin: at a mkd tree by a Swampe side from
               thence running for the Easterne bounds N by W $\frac{1}{2}$ point Wly
over the fourth run 240 po thence for the Northern bounds W by N 324 po
for the Westerne bounds SE by E $\frac{1}{2}$ point Ely 282 po then for the Southern
bounds East running through the sd fourth run & through a Swamp unto the

Swamps North Easterne side 162 po thence running S Eward by & along the
Swamps side unto its first begining for the transportation of 8 persons
WM: JELLEN, THO: HALL, ANN BISHOP, CHOE KATE?, WM: STUDS, THO: APSTANDS,
ELLINOR SMITH, TERLOCK? CRAGO?

3 Oct 1671 - ~~RICHARD~~ WILLIAM CORNIX 1736 acres in the Parrish of Lyn-
   (p376)   haven in the County of Lower Norfolk and part thereof be-
               ing the CHINKAPEN RIDGE, the GRASSES GROWND and SALISBURY
PLAYNE and pt (part) thereof lying to the Norwood (Northward?) of CHIN-
KAPEN RIDGE bounded as follows vizt: begining at a Cipres stump which
is on the NE point of the BEAVOR DAMMS and thence runing W and by S 320
po and thence SE ½ a point Ely 40 po & thence S by E 580 po & thence E
by N 132 po & thence S by E 142 po & th E by S ½ a point Soly 100 po to
a white oake neare THUNDER BOLT PINE BRANCH and thence N by E ½ point
Ely 382 po & thence N by N ½ a point Wly 262 po to a red oake and Hiccory standing together & marked on the Northern side of a branch issueing into a CIPRESS SWAMP & thence runing by the CIPRESS SWAMP Southward
& another branch thereof Westward unto a mkd Gum at the head of the sd
other branch & then downe the Northerne side of the branch till it meet-
eth with a lyne drawne SE by E from the first station thence along that
line N by W to its first station. 890 acres hereof was formerly granted to the sd CORNIX by two pattents dated 24 Nov 1657 (Nugent pp 355 &
415): and the other 846 acres due (RICHARD is crossed out in record)
for transportation of 17 persons: JNO: LAWRENCE, RICH: DAVIS, MARY
EDWARDS, ARRABLE MARTIN, ANN BOW, ALEX: DANIEL?, BEN: COUNCELL, WM:
NEWPORT, JAMES STEVAN, JNO: AXSTEAD (o Apstead?), MARGT: HEATH, EDWD:
LEATH, OLIVER HALL, ELLEN JOHNSON, ANN SADLER, THO: LAMBERT, ANN WIL-
LIAMS. (Note: The names Heath and Leath are in the record as follows:
                               AGW)

3 Oct 1671 - MR. HENRY SPRATT 1100 acres in the Parrish of Lynhaven
   (p377)   in the County of Lower Norfolk & the Northern Side of
               BROAD CREEK beginning at a mkd pine on the Eastern side
of the mouth of a branch & running from thence by severall lines of mkd
trees drawn as first N 164 po & then E by N 36 po & then S by E 56 po &
then E by N 185 po & then NE by N 164 po & then SE by E 320 po & then
SW & by S 110 po to trees marked for YOUNG GEO: ffOWLERS land then along
these marked trees SE 67? po & then SW by S by a line drawne unto a
branch of the sd BROAD CREEK and then running downe the sd branch on the
NORTHEASTERN SIDE of the DAMS of BROAD CREEKE unto its first beginning.
600 acres formerly granted to BARTH: HOSKINS by pattent dated 10 Mar
1662/3 & by HOSKINS sold to the sd SPRATT & 300 acres due for trans. of
6 persons: HEN: SPRATT, HEN: SPRATT (sic), ISSABELLA SPRATT, SARA
SWORTEN?, JNO: GOLD, GEO: HARRELL (or ffARRELL). (1662/3 patent is not
in Nugent in Barth: Hoskins name, maybe it will come to light in the
Lower Norfolk County Records - AGW)

3 Oct 1671 - ? THOMAS BRANT ? - (this name could be almost anything,
   (p377)   the last letter of the surname is a blot of ink. It might
               even be GRANT instead of Brant or Brent. AGW) See the
following: (CLEMENT ?) 150 acres in Lower

14

Norfolk County on the NORTHERNE SIDE OF BROAD CREEK beginning at a mkd
Cedar on a point of land at the branch parting this land from RICHARD
HARGROVES land running from that Cedar N by W 190 po thence SW by W ½ a
point Wly 165 po thence SE a point Soly: unto the sd. BROAD CREEKE &
then by the Creek & branch side unto its first begin: the sd land being
due for transportation of 3 persons: WM: JELLS?   , THO: HALL,
ANN BISHOP.

3 Oct 1671 - THOMAS WOLFTON   450 acres in Lower Norfolk Co.
   (p377)   at the SEABOARD   SIDE betweene ROODED
             & CURRATUCK. 100 acres thereof being an Island
in the fresh ponds called PATIENCE and commonly called or knowne by the
name of WOOLFTONS   ISLAND, the other 350 acres beginning at a
marked tree & the   Southermost end of the said Island and th:
runing S by E ½ point Ely 320 po th: W ½ a point Noly 380 po & th: by a
right line unto the Southermost end of the sd Island the sd land being
due for transportation of nine persons: THO: WOOLSTON?, his wife, his
5 sones & his two daughters.   (Note: Could the word
Rooded above be a misspell   ing of RUDEE? AGW)

3 Oct 1671 - HENRY SMITH 300 acres in Parrish of Lynhaven in the Coun-
   (p378)   ty of Lower Norfolk on the Southerne side of the BROAD RUN
             & on the East side of a CIPRES (Cypress) SWAMP and bound-
ing on the Western pte (part) by the said CIPRES SWAMP and on the South
by a line of marked trees drawne from a marked white oak standing at
the side of the sd CIPRES SWAMP ESE 188 po & then for the Easterne
bounds NNE 200 po & then for the Northerne bounds WNW 202 po unto the
BROAD RUN & along the Easterne side of the said CIPRES SWAMP unto its
first beginning due for transportation of 6 persons: WM: GOLD, DUDLY
KEALE, JNO: NASH, EVAN a Frenchman, SARA PORTER, MARY WE(BER?) or WEBB.

3 Oct 1671 - WILLIAM EDWARDS 200 acres in Lower Norfolk County at &
   (p378)   about a path that leadeth from the EASTERNE BRANCH of
             ELIZABETH RIVER unto the NORTH RIVER being Inclosed East-
ward & Westward by two parralel lynes of marked trees drawne S ½ point
Ely & N ½ point Wly 320 po -(reed?)- Northward & Southward by two par-
ralell lynes of marked trees drawen (sic) E & W 100 po. Sd land due
for transportation of 4 persons: HEN:POMROY, JNO: JACKSON, ffRA:
HENSHAW, ffLORENCE POMROY.

3 Oct 1671 - BENONY BURROUGH 944 acres in Parrish of Lynhaven in Low-
   (p379)   er Norfolk County on BENNETTS CREEKE neare the head and
             on the Northerne side of the land of ADAM THOROWGOOD be-
ginning at a marked white oake standing on the Northerne side of a
branch near the head of BEAVOR POND which pond was formerly a Marsh
called NEEDHAMS MARSH and from the sd mkd white oake bounded by Severall lynes drawne as followeth first NE 140 po then NW ½ point Nly 215
po then W 15º 15 minutes Soly 177 po unto the land that was MR. LAMBERTS
then SSW 10 po then SW 140 po unto the corner of the land that was ADAM
THOROWGOODS & now WM: SMITHS and thence by the sd SMITHS mkd trees E
250 po unto a POINT OF LAND neare the head of a gutt where is a quarter

mkd pine and the runing of the South Westerne side of ye DAMS form(erly)
called NEEDHAMS MARSH unto the red white (sic) oake at the first beginning. 590 acres part hereof was formerly granted to ffRA: YARDLEY by
pattent dated 28 Jul 1648 (not in Nugent) & by sd YARDLEY sold & assigned to CHRISTOPHER BURROUGHS by an assignmt recorded in Lower Norfolk
County 1 Jun 1652 and now due to sd. Benoni BURROUGH as heire to his
decd. father. The other 354 acres was formerly granted to XPOFER
BURROUGH by pattent dated 7 Nov 1651 (see Nugent p 221) and now becomes
due to sd BENONY (sic) BURROUGH as his heire to XPOFER BURROUGH his decd
father.

3 Oct 1671 - WM: HANCOCK   700 acres in Lynnhaven Parrish in Lower Nor-
   (p379a)   folk County on the Northerne Side of the EASTERNE BRANCH
               of ELIZABETH RIVER and bounded on the Southerne parts
therewith and on the South Easterne side of a Creeke called HOSKINS CR.
pting this land from the land of MR. WM: MOSELEY beginning at a mkd
cedarstanding by the side of the said EASTERNE BRANCH and from thence
running by a line drawne NNE 202 po and then by a line drawne NE 3º Ely
150 po and then E 259 po & then NNE 100 po & then WNW 400 po & then SSW
80 po & then ESE 104 po & then SSW 142 po & then WNW 160 po unto the
Creeke called HOSKINS CREEKE & then downe the South Easterne side of sd
Creeke unto its mouth at the Easterne Branch and then South Eastwood
runing up the sd Easterne branch unto the Cedar where it began and
100 acres pt hereof was formerly granted to GEO: ffOWLER by pattent
dated 6 Nov 1663 and by sd. ffOWLER sold & assigned to the sd WM: HAN-
COCK and the other 600 acres is due for trans of 12 persons: MARY &
HENRY SLADE, CHARLES BAKER, ELIZ: VOUSE, JNO: REE, JNO: QUELCY, JAYNE
JOFLIN (or Joslin), CHARLES REGARALL, WM: RICHARDSON, JNO: COOKE, BARTH:
SHOAE, TEAGE at (or et) DOVELL. (Nugent 539 26 Nov 1663)

4 Oct 1671 - CHARLES GRANDY   366 acres in Lower Norfolk County upon
   (p380)   the NORTH SIDE of DANIEL TANNERS CREEKE.   46 acres be-
              ginning at a mkd pine thence running NNE 160 po to
another mkd pine thence ESE 46 po to a Creeke side thence SSW 160 po to
a mkd pine soe WNW 40 po to the first station.
              320 acres beginning at a mkd pine joyneing to the North
side of the aforesd 46 acres of land and runing N 160 po to a mkd red
oake thence E 320 po bounding upon COLL: MASONS land -(faded)- xx xxxx
and soe away S 160 po to a mkd white oake joyneing to the land of MICH:
LAWRENCE and from th: W 320 po downe the creeke to the first station sd
land due for transportation of 8 persons: WM: CHICHESTER, his wife,
foure children, JNO: REESE, THO: LEONARD.

27 Oct 1670 - WM: CORNISH   550 acres in Northumberland County
   (p382)

29 Sep 1671 - WM: MOSELEY & RICH: CATLETT   1700 acres of land in
   (p384)   Rappahannock County.

27 Oct 1670 - THOMAS HARDING   520 acres in Northumberland County. (this
   (p385)   patent is too faded to read.)

5 Nov 1671 - CHRISTOPHER BUSTIAN 660 acres in the SOUTHERNE BRANCH of
   (p385)   ELIZABETH RIVER in Lower Norfolk County beginning at a
              mkd oake standing on the banke of the said River and run-
ing West by S ½ Soly butting on MARKHAMS land now in possession of GEO:
VALLENTINE 275 po to a mkd red oake and from thence N by W ½ Wly 285 po
to a mkd pine being the corner tree of CAPT: WM: CARNERS land thence
ENE 38 po to a mkd gum in a pond thence N by E 52 po to another gum in
a branch of a Creeke runing between the land of CAPT: CARVER & CHRIST-
OPHER BUSTIAN thence Downe the said branch and Creeke on Severall
courses to the mouth of the same Creeke and soe along the side of the
said Southerne Branch xxxxxx xxxxxxx (left side of page is practical-
ly faded out) to the first mentioned mkd tree.
              450 acres of the sd land being formerly granted to JOHN
YATES by him sold to JAMES WARNER and by sd WARNER sold and assigned
to the said XPOFER BUSTIN (sic) the remainder being 210 acres is land
within the said bounds and due for transportation of 5 persons: JNO:
LAWSON, MARY BRUCE, WM: LEMRIDGE?   ROBT: BEMIS, xxExxx
JOHNSON.

__ Mar 1671 - CAPT: JOHN WEST 3650 acres in NoHampton County. (This
   (p391)   patent is too faded to read)

23 Mar 1671/2- CAPT: JNO: WEST, CHA: SCARBURGH & DEBORAH BROWN 4500
   (p398)   acres of land in Northampton County.

28 Oct 1672 - CAPT: THOMAS FULCHER 60 acres in Lower Norfolk County
   (p407)   formerly granted to CAPT: ROBERT PAGE and lately found
               to escheat to his maties &c......Bounds are not given.

28 Oct 1672 - MALACHY THRUSTON 100 acres according to the ancient
   (p408)   bounds in Lower Norfolk County and formerly granted
               to WILLIAM HOLLEY & found to escheat &c...............

28 Oct 1672 - BARTHEW: WILLIAMSON 110 acres in Lower Norfolk County
   (p408)   according to the antient (sic) lawfull bounds formerly
               granted to ROBERT WORSTER (Foster?)
and is lately found to escheat &c................................(this
name should be ffOSTER. It has been found in other records spelled
this same way) (Note: there is no patent to Richard Worster in Nugent,
however there are several to RICHARD FOSTER. AGW)

28 Oct 1672 - MRS. KATHERINE LAWRENCE 160 acres in Lower Norfolk
   (p408)   County according to the ancient bounds and was formerly
               granted to THOMAS GREGORY and lately found to escheat...
..................&c...(The Gregory patent is not in Nugent)

28 Oct 1672 - AUGUSTINE MOORE 225 acres in ELIZABETH CITY COUNTY
   (p408)   formerly granted to THOMAS SHIRLEY and lately found to
               escheat &c........(Shirley patent not in Nugent)

28 Oct 1672 - THOMAS TABB 300 acres in ELIZABETH CITY COUNTY according
   (p408)   to the ancient bounds formerly granted to JOHN GIBBS

and is lately found to escheat &c...........(Nugent p 98: JOHN GIBBS
300 acres Eliza: City Co. 27 Sep 1638 bounded on S by land of THOMAS
PURIFYE & on the W by land of THOMAS SEWELL.........)

1 Jul 1672 - RICHARD JONES, MARINER 680 acres in the SOUTHERNE BRANCH
   (p409)   of ELIZABETH RIVER on ye East side thereof. 400 acres part
              thereof beginning at a mkd pine standing by a Creeke side
and running for breadth So E 100 po to a mkd pine standing by a SANDY
POINT by another Creeke by the MAYNE RIVER to a mkd white oak standing
on a SANDY POINT by another Creeke and from thence NE into the woods
320 po to a mkd white oak thence NW 200 po to a mkd white oak soe SW
320 po to the first mentioned station.
              280 acres the residue of the sd 680 acres adjoyning begin-
ning at a mkd pine standing on the So side of a Creeke and running a-
long the MAINE RIVER S by E 140 po to a Black Walnut tree and from th:
so East by E along the river 68 po to a mkd hicory standing on a point
on the North side of another Creeke and so over the branch into the
woods E by N 120 po to a mkd Pine standing by a branch side th: N ½ Ely
224 po to a marked pine standing on a swamp side th: NW 60 po to a mkd
Spanish Oake standing in the Swamp and from th: WSW 205 po to the first
station. The first 400 acres being part of a p ttent formerly taken up
by one MR. WM: JULYAN and by fower conveyances i last becomes due to
sd RICHARD JOANES (see Nugent p 48)
              The other 280 acres being due by pattent dated 8 Apr 1665.
(See Nugent p 445 Mr. Richard Jones patent for 300 acres 28 Apr 1665 at
the head of the S. Br of Eliza Riv.)

28 Oct 1673 - JNO: KENDALL 200 acres in ACCOMAC.............. mkd trees
   (p413)   of JNO: WALTER.............land of THOMAS BELL...........
              land of MAJOR JNO: TYLINEY?; ....first granted to
COL: WM: KENDALL by patent dated 6 Oct 1670.........& by him deserted
......head rights: ROBT: ARMSTRONG, JNO: JOHNSON, ALICE BRUISE, JAMES
HENDERSON.

8 Oct 1672 - THOMAS COTTELL 50 acres in WESTERN BRANCH of ELIZ: RIVER
   (p417)   joyning to a former parcell of land of the said COTTLES
              beginning at a mkd Pohickery standing by the branch side
and running for length NW 320 po and soe againe from the first mentioned tree for breadth NE 25 Po abutting on the land of ROBERT GRIMES and
so againe for length NW 320 po to a mkd pyne standing in the MAINE
SWAMP concluding and bounding the said land which is due for transportation of one person: ELIZABETH HIDE.

1 Oct 1672 - DENNIS DALLY (this name is DAWLEY a Norfolk County name)
   (p419)   200 acres in Lower Norfolk County in LYNNHAVEN begin: at
              ye SEABOARD SIDE at a mkd Poplar by the head of a branch
running SW 100 po to a mkd Pohickey th: NW 320 po to the head of the
BEAVER DAMMS and th: NE 100 (or 400?) po to a line of trees....the
land of CAPPS & th: SE 224 po along the land of CAPT: LAWRENCE to the
first station the said land being due for transportation of four persons: ELIZABETH WATKINS, ELLENOR EDWARDS, WM: DAVISON, DANIELL FRISELL.

1 Oct 1672 - DENNIS DALLY (DAWLEY) 600 acres in Lower Norfolk County
   (p419)   at the head of the EASTERNE SHORE of LINHAVEN beginning
               at a mkd tree on the SHORE RIDGE thence running SW by W
by a line of mkd trees 570 po to a corner mkd tree thence WNN ½ Nly by
a line of mkd trees 134 po to another corner mkd tree neere to the land
of EDMOND MOORE thence NE by another line of mkd trees 440 po to another corner tree thence E ½ Northly to MR: WM: BROCKS branch and thence
by the sd branch to the first station due for transportation of 12 persons: ROBERT BRAY 3 tymes, JOHN KINES?, MARY WOOD, XOFAND (Roland? the
X is an X?) ROBEY, MORGAN BRYAN, WALTER POWELL, ELIZABETH SMITH & 3
negroes.

29 Sep 1672 - WILLIAM NICCOLLS 350 acres in Lower Norfolk County upon
   (p420)   the SOUTH SIDE of the EASTERNE BRANCH of·ELIZA: RIV:
               called LYONS QUARTER beginning at a mkd white oake thence
running into the woods by a line of mkd trees SE by S 320 po to a mkd
Beech thence SW by W 160 po to another beech by a run side thence NW by
W 320 po to the head of a Neck so NE by E 160 po to the place where it
began. Due for transportation of seaven persons: 3 negroes - JONE,
MARY, KATHERINE; 2 negroes - THOMAS, PETER; 1 negro ELLENO & RICHD:
BARRETT.

1 Oct 1672 - ALEX GUIN or GUYN (spelled both ways in patent) 186 3/4
   (p420)   acres in Lower Norfolk County in DANIEL TANNERS CREEK be-
               ginning at a mkd white oake and from thence by a line of
mkd trees SE 166 po to a marker rods (rod?) standing at the head of a
branch so NE 180 po into the Swamp to a marked oake so along the POCO-
SONS NW 166 po to a Gum thence SW 180 po to the first station due for
transportation of 4 persons: THO: LAMBERT, ANN WILLIAMS(on ?), ROBERT
HARPER, JAMES LOWMAN (or Bowman?)

30 Sep 1672 - ROBERT YOUNG of Elizabeth River in Lower Norfolk County.
   (p422)   250 acres in Lynnhaven Parrish in Lower Norfolk begin:
               at a mkd Pine on a Poynt by a Small Branch runing into
the BROAD CREEKE thence SE by S 125 po to a mkd Pine thence SW by W
320 po to a mkd pine thence NW by N 125 po to the BROAD CREEK & by ye
BROAD CREEK 320 po to ye first station.....sd 250 acres being formerly
granted to xxx THO: BROWN by pattent dated -blot- Mar 1652 and by his
liberall assignmts at last came to ye sd ROBERT YOUNG. (see Nugent 273)

3 Apr 1673 - JOHN WEST 2500 acres in Northampton County, another patt:
   (p423)   for 1000 acres and another for 500 acres. All in same
               County, same date and page.

4 Oct 1673 - COL: JOHN STRINGER 400 acres in Northampton County
   (p424)   formerly Accomack.....................................

24 Oct 1673 - CHAS: & MARY CALVERT 800 acres in Northampton County.
   (p434)   Formerly granted to XPOFER CALVERT 2 Oct 1655 (see Nugent
               p 322)

9 Oct 1672 - RICHARD BAILY 1200 acres in Northampton County. 700 acs.
   (p434)   formerly granted to RICHARD BAILY the father by patt: 15
               Sep 1649 & now due to RICHARD BAILY as hyre to his father.
The other 500 acres not granted TILY NORTON by patt: 24 Jul 1651 &
by him assigned to RICHARD BAILY decd .....&c............................
(see Nugent p 217: TOBY NORTON 500 acres Northampton County 24 Jul
1651, at Corratock Creek & bounded on the Southern part by sd Cr. & land
of RICHARD BAYLEY.)

9 Oct 1672 - RICHARD KELLAM 1850 acres in Northampton County.
   (p434)

11 Nov 1672 - WM: WHITTINGTON 2850 acres in NORTHTON (Northampton?) Co.
   (p439)   att HUNGARS............... THOMAS MIDDLETON one of the
               headrights.......

5 Sep 1672 - WM: DRUMMOND 960 acres in Lower Norfolk County upon the
   (p444)   EAST SIDE of the BRANCH of the NORTH RIVER of COROTOCKE.
               Beginning at a mked Cypress tree standing in a GREATE
CYPRESS SWAMP & running NNE by a line of mkd trees up the said Swamp
320 po to a mkd red oake and from th: by a line of mkd ESE 320 po to a
mkd pine tree standing in the woods and from thence SSW by another line
of mkd trees 640 po to a mkd Gum which standeth in a small Swamp which
faceth a branch of the said River and so up the said branch being Reduct?
(reduced?) to a Right line NNW to the first station. Due for trans: of
20 persons: JAS: BISHOP, 4 negroes, JNO: CREWES, RICHD: MUMPTON, MARY
COFFINS, SAM: HALCOT?, JNO: HALL, WM: DUNTON, MATH: WILKINSON, JNO: SMITH,
WM: DAWLEY, RICH: CEELY, JA: STRADLING, MATH: NASH, WM: DAVIS, WM: GRACE.

8 May 1673 - CHARLES BLANKEVILE 440 acres in WARWICK COUNTY.....neare
   (p450)   the Banke of JAMES RIVER........MR. STRATTON(s) land now
               in the tenure of MR. THO: MERRY.......butting SE on the
land of SYMON DANIELLS orphans now in possession of JNO: JACKSON.......
sd. land due as followeth: formerly in the possession of HEN: MOORE decd
whose relict the said CHARLE(s) BANKEVILE (sic) married & is further due
for transportation of 9 persons. (Names not given)

13 May 1673 - JOHN HATTON 240 acres in Lower Norfolk County xxx (on?)
   (p451)   the WESTERNE BRANCH of ELIZA: RIVER and beginning att a
               pine at the mouth of a Swamp issuing out of LANGLEY CREEK
& running N butting on the land of STEPHEN MARKS 320 po unto the Swamp
thence West 114 po to a certaine mkd tree in the same Swamp thence S
350 po to a pine on the West side of the Mouth of a Creek parting this
from the lande late COLL: BRONE   thence along the said LANGLIES
CREEKE to the first marked tree.   The land being pcell of 300
acres formerly granted to the sd JOHN HATTON by patt: dated 11 Jan 1652
and is now renewed. (see Nugent p 269 - JOHN HATTON 300 acres in the
Westermost branch of Eliz. Riv. near the head of BROWNS CREEK 11 Jan 1652

13 May 1673 - JOHN WILKISON & THO: WRIGHT among head rights in patent to
   (p452)   JOHN DUKE 486 acres in James City County.

28 Mar 1672 - WM: WILSON 300 acres in Lower Norfolk County at the head
   (p453)   of a branch of Elizabeth River beginning at a white oake
                 standing by a Run of Water & runing South 220 po to a mkd
pine standing by a swampside and soe running West along the side of a
Swamp 320 po and soe N 80 po to a run and soe runing down by or nigh the
run ENE to the first station. Sd land being formerly granted to RICH:
JONES by patt: dated 28 Apr 1665 & by him deserted and is now granted to
the said WM: WILSON &c....and for the transportation of 6 persons:
MATHEW BENTLEY, ROBERT GREENE, RICH: ffORTICE, THOS: SWANN, ELIZABETH
STAFFORD, JNO: (RIVER?)   (See Nugent 445 Richard Jones and
6 PB 409 and page 18   of these notes)

27 May 1673 - MATHEW SHIPP 400 acres in Lower Norfolk County it being
   (p456)   a NECK OF LAND whose Point shoots? against the Up(p)er
               Landing of the NORTH RIVER. Bounded North Eastward &
South Westward by two pocosons and running NW into the woods. Due for
transportation of 8 persons: EDW: SMITH, JNO: SMITH, JNO: SPRATT, THO:
RICHARDSON, MARIE ffOX, EDW: STILES, ELINER HALL, JA: COLEMAN.

27 May 1673 - JOHN LADD 700 acres in Lower Norfolk County in Linhaven
   (p456)   Pish on both sides of LINHAVEN RIVER neare its head and
                on the South Westward side of BEAVER DAMS and its Creeke
& bounded on the NEward parts therewith begining at a mkd tree by a
path and by a branch above the head of the Dams thence running by severall line of mkd trees Drawne as followeth first SSW 40 po then WSW
102 po then NNW 40 po then WSW 102 po then NNW 40 po then WSW 180 po
crossing the head of the river then NNW 200 then ENE 400 po unto the
DEEP BRANCH which is on the NW side of the river then downe the said
DEEP BRANCH unto the end and Downe the River unto the mouth of the
BEAVER DAM CREEKE thence up the Creeke, Dams and its Branch unto the
first beginning...
                600 acres part hereof was granted to MR: EDW: HALL by
patt: dated the 30 Jun 1661 and by the said HALL 300 acres part of his
600 acres was the 16 May 1663 assigned to SAVILL GASKINS & by JOB
GASKIN sonn & heire of the said SAVELL GASKINS was the 10 May 1671 assigned unto the said JNO: LADD.
                The other 300 acres being another part of the said 600
acres was the 5 Jan 1663 by EDW: HALL assigned to ROGER ffOUNTAINE &
by him was the 28 Aug 1665 assigned to JNO: BORING & by the said BOR-
ING by bill of sale 11 Oct 1670 sold unto sd JNO: LADD.
                The 100 acres residue for transportation of 2 persons:
JAMES KING and THO: MAY.

27 May 1673 - JACOB JOHNSON 600 acres in Lower Norfolk County in
   (p457)   LINHAVEN PARISH at a branch of LITTLE CREEK bounded on ye
                NW on ye sd branch of LITTLE CREEK (Lake Smith?) & runing
from ye same ENE 200 po along by ye land that was formerly MR. GRIGGINS
            land and beyond it thence NNW 104 po to ye land of LT.
                COL. ADDAM THOROWGOOD thence NNW ½ W 46 po thence SSW 50
po thence WNW 310 po to ye sd br. of LITTLE CREEK then running by ye sd
branch to ye first beginning.
                400 acres hereof is part of 500 acres granted to ROBERT

21

HAYES by pattent dated 22 Nov 164(8?) & by NATHANIEL and ADDAM HAYES
sonnes of ye sd ROBT: HAYES sold to MR. SYMON CORNIX decd & by WM:
CORNIX sonne & heire of ye sd SIMON CORNIX sold to MR. ROBT: BRAY &
by ye sd BRAY sold to ye sd JACOB JOHNSON.

      100 acres another part granted to ROWL'D: MORGAN by patt:
dated 8 Nov 1651 & by ye sd MORGAN sold to WM: HANN (or ffANN) & by ye
sd HANN sold to WM: JOHNSON and by JOHNSON sold to MR. SYMON CORNIX
& BY WM: CORNIX sonne & heire to ye sd SYMOND (sic) CORNIX sold to MR.
ROBT: BRAY & by ye sd BRAY to ye sd JACOB JOHNSON.

      100 acres ye residue due by transportation of 2 persons:
JACOB JOHNSON for himselfe twice.

      (Nugent p 182 - Mr. ROBERT HAYES 500 acres Low. Norf. Co.
22 Nov 1648 ...on the Southermost branch of LITTLE CREEK in Linhaven
Parish beg: at CRAINE MARSH POINTetc. along land of CAPT. JOHN GOOKIN,
decd., & by ADAM THOROGOODS land......250 acs by patent dated 28 Sep
1643 & the other 50 acres for trans: of one person.)

      (Nugent p 221 - ROWLAND MORGAN 100 acres Linhaven Parish
Low: Norf: Co. in the Dam. Neck 8 Nov 1651. Bounded on the Western
side with land of NATHANIELL HAYES on S side with the BEAVER DAM &
thence runing NE by E etc.) (Note:- This must be same land and the
Dam. Neck in Nugent must mean the Beaver Dams? AGW)

27 May 1673 - ffRANCIS SHIPP 550 acres in Lower Norfolk County being
  (p458)   a necke of land made by the turnings of a CYPRESS SWAMP
       & bounded on ye SW, SE and NE by ye conjunction of ye
sd Swamp with ye woodland Ground & bounded NWly by a line of marked
trees drawen (sic) NE by E 248 po cross ye sd neck ye sd land due to
sd SHIPP for transportation of 11 persons: JACOB JOHNSON for trans-
porting himselfe 4 tymes, JOHN SYMONS, JAMES KIRKWOOD, THO: BURNETT,
ROSE RUSSELL, JONATHAN GARNETT, SARA OWIN, -blank- BURFIELD.

27 May 1673 - BENIO BORACE (BENONNE BORACE which is meant to be
  (p458)   BENNONY BURROUGHS)
      994 acres of land in
LINHAVEN in Lower Norfolk County in BENNETTS CREEK near its head & on
ye Northern side of ye land formerly ADDAM THOROWGOODS beginning at a
mkd Pohickarie standing at NEEDHAMS MARSH neer THO: DAVIS his fence
& from thence bounded by several lines drawne as followeth: first
NW ½ Nly 285 po to ye land that was MR. LAMBERTS then SW 136 po then
S by W 306 po then E 13° Nly 292 po to the corner of the land formerly
ADDAM THOROWGOODS & now WM: SMITHS thence by ye sd SMITHS mked trees
252 po to a poynt of land neer ye head of a Gutt where is a marked
Quarter Pine thence running by ye sd NEEDHAMS MARSH unto against ye
first beginning, then over ye DAMS to the first beginning (sic).
      944 acres hereof granted to ye sd BORACE by pattent
dated 30 Oct 1671 & the other 50 due for trans: of one person: THO:
IVY.   (See page 15 of these notes Benony Burrough & 6 PB 379)

27 May 1673 - JOHN TAYLOR 34 acres in ACCOMAC COUNTY for transporta-
  (p458)   tion of one person: THO: IVY the second time.

27 May 1673 - RICH: ffOUNDER 100 acres in Lower Norfolk County at
   (p458)   LITTLE CREEK between a Branch of ye sd Creek on ye East
             & ye mkd trees commonly called MR. THOROWGOODS GRAND
PATTENT on ye NE and the land that was formerly ROBT: HAYES land on ye
South it being ye land that said FOUNDER lives on. Said land due for
transportation of 2 persons: JNO: LESTRANGE & WM: (ACHAN?)

27 May 1673 - WM: WEST 400 acres in Lower Norfolk County in ye woods
   (p459)   neer the NORTH RIVER & on the Westerne side of a GREAT
             POQUOSON bounded on ye Eastern parts therewith beginn-
ing at ye side thereof runing from thence by marked trees drawne W
274 po then SW 68 po then S 126 po then SSE 96 po then ENE 244 po to
ye sd POQUOSON ye sd land due for transportation of 8 persons: JNO:
JAMES, ABRAHAM JOHNSON, PETER VINTON, JEFFREY AYRES, WM: PEENE?
ALICE MOON, ROBT: WILLS, WM: DIRKE.

Note:- This Court Clerk is careless. He leaves letters as well as
whole words out. AGW

27 May 1673 - ffINLAW MACKWILLIAM 400 acres in Northampton County for
   (p459)   transportation of 8 persons: JNO: AYRES eight tymes.
             (This shows that the year of a patent does not necessar-
ily mean that the headrights arrived in that specific year. Jno: Ayres
must have first come to the Colonies at least 8 years before this patent in 1673. But - If he had come from Barbadoes or Bermuda those
7 or 8 tymes his trips may have been closer together. AGW)

27 May 1673 - RICH: KELLAM 1000 acres in Northampton County neer land
   (p460)   of MR. JNO: WEST & RICH: BAYLEY.   850 acres was formerly
             granted to KELLAM 9 Nov 1666.
   (p461)   Same date - 1850 acres in Northampton County.

28 May 1673 - RICH: BONNE (BONNEY?) 1300 acres in Lower Norfolk Co.
   (p462)   beginning at a GREAT POSSOSON of the NORTH RIVER & run-
             ing from thence by a line of mkd trees drawne E by S 184
po & then NNE 610 po & NNW ½ point Wly 316 po then WSW ½ Sly 224 po
and then SSE ½ Ely 210 po & then SSW 576 po into the Poccoson & then
East and by South 79 po unto the first beginning including unto these
bounds the   (part) of COW QUARTERIDGE.
land being due   for   transportation of 26 persons: JNO: D.
JAMES, JNO: MARTOONE, ELIZ: TOM, ROBT: TRAYLE (or GRAYLE), WM: RUSSELL,
ELIZ: KING, THO: VINCE, EDW: GEORGE, JEFF BEAKE, HUGH ffARGISON (Fergu-
son) HUGH CROOKE, PENOLOPE CASE, THRUSTON MAYO, JNO a French Boy, PAT-
RICK a Irish boy, HANNAH VINCE, JA: HARTLESTE?, JAMES MORRILL, THOMAS
RUSSELL, JAMES ASHTON, SARAH SHILLING, NICH: LACKLAND, JNO: BUTTON, EDM.
BASKEY, JNO: HARRIS, THO: Rxxxxxed (REDGNOLD?)

28 May 1673 - DEARMAN MACKELL (MacCALL?) 100 acres in Lower Norfolk Co.
   (p462)   neare RUDEE between the SALT PONDS on the West and the
             SAND BANCKS on the Seaboard side on the East and running
from a white oake neare the head of (a) branch of the SALT PONDS NNE

Easterly (sic) 47 po then East 106 (po) to the SAND BANKS unto a branch
of the SALT PONDS. Due for transportation of 2 persons: THO: DEANE &
THO: BENCH.

28 May 1673 - JNO: ffRIZLE 100 acres of land on the SEABOARD two? (to)
   (p462)   the Northward of RUDEE in Lower Norfolk County bounded
               Eastward on the SAND BANCKS Southward on the mkd trees of
the land of DEARMAN MACKELES and from the said MACKELES corner tree
bounded by mkd trees Drawne N by W ½ Wly 140 po and then East unto the
SAND BANCKS. The said land being due for transportation of 2 persons:
OWEN WILES & BRIGETT JEROME.

14 Jul 1673 - JOHN CORPOCYON? *Corporyon*   100 acres in Pish of Lynn:
   (p464)   in Lower Norfolk County in the woods betweene the Easterne
               and Southern Branches of ELIZABETH RIVER bounding /on the
marked trees/ Eastward upon the land of the WHITEHUSTS and Southward by
a line of mked trees drawne from the WHITEHUSTS Southern Corner trees
E by S 28 po unto the land of DAVID MURROW. Due for transportation of
2 persons: ELINOR EDWARDS and a Trumpeter.

14 Jul 1673 - JOHN CORPREW 500 acres in Lower Norfolk County beginning
   (p464)   at a mkd pine standing by the side of a Swamp called
               RIDGEFORD SWAMP on the head of the SOUTHERNE BRANCH of
Elizabeth River at a place called the BEARE? SPRING (*beare*) and
running downe the said Swamp E by N 330 po to a mkd red oake neare the
mouth of a branch falling into the same Swamp then bounding on the said
Swamp 243 po to another mkd oake thence W by S 330 po to a Pine thence
N by W 243 po to the first menconed place by the said RIDGEFORD SWAMP
side including and bounding the said 500 acres. Due for transportation
of 10 persons: a DUTCH body, ELINOR DIKE, DANIELL SULIVANT (or Suli-
bant), JNO: NORRIS, WM: PANGBORNE, DANIELL *Afonzja* ? , 3 negroes

24 Aug 1660 (crossed out in Patent and 1673 inserted) - JOHN WILLIAMS
   (p465)   444½ acres in Lower Norfolk County upon the SOUTH SIDE of
               DANIELL TANNERS CREEKE beginning at a cedar post by a
stump of his thence by a line of mkd trees NW 108 po to the land of
ABRAHAM ELLETT & RICHARD JOANES & from thence on a line of mkd trees
140 po to a mkd pine joyning to the land of WM: COOPER thence SE 508 po
to his formar devident thence SW 140 po to the first station due for
transportation of 9 persons: PHILLIP HAMBLIN, ROBERT HALSEY, JOHN DUNN,
HENRY EWBANKS (Eubanks?), CHRISTOPHER FLEMING, EDW: BO_ARDLER? JOHN
BUTLER, THO: (can't read, too faded).

8 Aug 1673 - JAMES WESHARD (This name is Wishard, the modern counter-
   (p466)   part is Whichard) 200 acres in Lower Norfolk County nere
               the PINE NECK DAMS which belongs to LITTLE CREEK begining
at a mkd tree of ANN BENNETTS land standing neare the head of a branch
of the said DAMS & alsoe neare to the HIGH ROADE from thence runing
first SW by W ½ W 246 po then NNW ¼ W 90 po then NE 133 po then ESE ¼ E
170 po unto the first beginning and againe from the first beginning
runing first E by N 120 po then S by E ½ E 80 po then W by S 108 po un-

to the aforesd DAMS and then up the Easterne side of the Dams unto the
first beginning. Due for transportation of 4 persons: AMBROS CURTIS,
NICH: HUGGENS, FLORENCE CARTER, WILLM: GRIFFIN.

23 Oct 1673 - DANIELL MACOY 189 acres in Lower Norfolk County on ye
   (p470)   EAST SIDE of the SOUTHERNE BRANCH of Elizabeth River be-
               gining at a mkd red oake on the N side of the LITTLE
CREEKE it being the Corner tree of ALEXANDER ROSTERS (ROYSTER?) land
and soe running thence by the said ROSTERS line South 76 po to another
mkd oake then S by W 42 po to a mkd white oake in a Swamp then S 22 po
to a Black Gum in the said Swamp thence SE 40 po to a mkd Pine then
E 3/4 S 105 po then ENE 50 po to a gum standing in the Path that goeth
to old BUTTS then ENE ½ E 80 po to a mkd holley & from thence N 36 po
to a Black Gum at the head of the said Creeke then downe by the said
Creeke NNW 257 po to the first mentioned tree. Land being due sd MACOY
as followeth: 100 acres thereof being formerly granted to THO: HALL by
Patt: about 30th (sic)yeares since and by severall conveyances made
over to ye said MACOY & 89(acres) the residue by & for the transportation of 2 persons: GEO: IVEY, HANNA IVEY.

23 Oct 1673 - RICH: JONES SENR: 400 acres in Lower Norfolk County be-
   (p471)   ginning at a marked pine standing one (on) a point soe
               running up by BOWMANS RUNN S by W 320 pole to a mkd DOGG
Tree (Dogwood tree?) by ye Runn side soe E by S 200 po to a mkd oake
soe N by E 320 po to a mkd pine soe up by runn side W by N 200 po to
the first station. The land is due for transportation of 8 persons:
ELINOR HARRINGTON, JNO: MOSS, KATHERINE WOOD, JA: CODDER, MODLING BAR-
RON, OWEN DOGHERTY, NICH: GILLINE, ROBT: SMART.

23 Oct 1673 - DENNAS MACOY 160 acres in Lower Norfolk County, said
   (p471)   land is due to ye said MACOY as followeth: 60 acres or
               thereabout being part of a patt: granted to THO: ETHE-
RIDGE 10 (Nov?) 1649 by severall Conveyances made over to the said
MACOY and 100 acres for transportation of 2 persons it being in Lower Norfolk County joyning to the sd land on the East side of the
SOUTHERNE BRANCH of Elizabeth River. Begin at a mkd Gum and fro(m)
thence running 100 po by said line 15 po into the said Swamp then
NW by N 189 po then SW by W 81 po then SE by S 149 po & then S by W
56 po to ye first station. THO: JENKINS, JNO: CHAPMAN.

23 Oct 1673 - JNO: WALLIS 330 acres in Lower Norfolk County on the
   (p471)   WEST SIDE of the SOUTHERNE BRANCH of Elizabeth River be-
               ginning at a mkd Cedar at the mouth of JULIANS CREEKE &
from thence runing 80 po NE then N 145 po to ye land of EDWD: DAVIS
from thence W along the said DAVIS line 310 po to a mkd Pine in a
Swamp and from thence 580 po then SW 50 po to an old mkd Pine standing on a point in JULIANS CREEKE and soe downe the said Creeke E by S
½ S 306 po to the first station. The said land being due as followeth
vizt: 200 acres or thereabouts being formerly granted to CAPT: WM:
CARVER by Patt: p (for) 500 acres bearing date 5 Jun 1654 (or 1659?) &
renewed in his Maties: name 4 Jul 1664 & by ye said CARVER sold to the
said WALLIS 15 Jun 1666 & 130 ye residue for trans: of 3 psons: a negro

& 2 Indians. (Note:- Why was credit given for Indians as head rights?
Weren't there enough here already? AGW) (For Carver patent see Nugent
p 477 "200 acres beg: near the mouth of Julians Creeke. Renewal dated
15 Jun 1659").

23 Oct 1673 - WARREN GODFREY & ISAAC BARRENTON 204 acres in Lower Nor-
   (p471)   begining pt (part?) of the RIDGE of land being betweene
              the EASTERNE & SOUTHERNE BRANCHES of ELIZABETH RIVER Be-
gining at a mkd pine nere unto ANTHONY BENFORDS land & from theare (sic)
by a line of mkd trees E SE 122 po to another mkd pine standing in a
POCOSON & from thence alongst the said Pocoson to the line (of) EVAN
WILLIAMS land NNE 269 po and soe along the sd land NNW 150 po & fro(m)
thence SSW 371 po to the first menconed mkd trees. The said land being
due for trans: of 5 psons: Bess, Sambo, Mingo, Jack, Betty - Negroes.

23 Oct 1673 - HEN: SPRATT 1800 acres in Lower Norfolk County it being
   (p472)   a NECK OF LAND in CURRATUCK Betw: (between) NANERS CREEKE
              on the South, a Little Creeke on the N running Wly into
the Woods including all the marshes betw: the said Creekes. The said
land being due for trans: of 36 psons: Himselfe 6 times, THO: ROGERS,
BRIDGER MILLCAHY?, RICHD: PLEDG, THO: NASH, CATE GREARE (Kate Gary?),
Jack, Little Jack, Indian Hanna, Moreia & a child, Negroes, JNO: CHAM-
BERLIN his wife, ELIZ: CARVER, ROSE CARVER, fine Nan, RICHD: PAINE,
RICHD: TAYLOR, EDMUND SHOULDER, ELIZ: GARLAND, MARY PARR, WM: SMITH,
THO: WHITTBY, WM: JONSON, NICH: NICHOLSON, HEN: SPICER, HERMAN MAIRE,
CORE? JOHNS, PAULE RAMERS, PETER LINHALL. (Note;- This is a good
example showing that the patents were not always dated when the head
rights were newly arrived in the Colony. Thos: Nash & Richard Taylor
were on former patents together, one in 1665 (Nugent 565) and Thos:
Nash was decd in February 1672/3 or before, as his Inventory and
apprenticeship of his son Thomas is in the Lower Norfolk County Records
in Book E - both in Feb 1672/3. Your editor has seen other patents
which seem to be dated some years after the head rights arrived. Some
of these head rights may well have taken a trip home, but not all of
them. AGW).

23 Oct 1673 - MICHAELL ffENTRIS 450 acres in Lower Norfolk County on
   (p472)   the SOUTH SIDE of the EASTERNE BRANCH of Elizabeth River
beginning at a corner of THO: CARTRIGHTS land thence S by E 250 po then
SSW 170 po then SW 3/4 Sly 228 po unto the mkd trees of the land of
WM: NICKLIS (Nicholls?) then along the mkd trees of the sd NICKLIS land
& the land of EVAN WILLIAM NW by N 302 po unto the mkd trees of the
(cleared?) land of HENRY NICKLIS (Henry Nicholls land near THO: CARTRIGHT
land S side of the E. Br. of Eliz. Riv. Nugent p 564) then along his
mkd trees first E by S ½ S 180 po then N 240 po to a corner tree then
E by N 174 po to the first station. 300 acres part thereof being formerly granted to MANASLEY PORTER by Patt: 15 Jan 1661 and descended to
his brother & heire JNO: PORTER SENR: & by the said JNO: PORTER sould
to the (said) MICH: ffENTRIS & his heires by assigmt: dated 28 Sep 1632
(sic) and by bill of sale of the land dated as may appeare upon LNco
records 17 Feb ffolling (following?) & 150 acres the residue for trans:
of 3 psons: WM: ELIS, ELIZ: HOOKER & one Negroe.

23 Oct 1673 - JNO: THROWER *Thrower* 100 acres in Lower Norfolk County
   (p472)   Joyning upon   a creeke called COL: MASON LITTLE
            CREEK on ye side and the land of CAPT: THO: FULCHER accord-
ing to the ancient bounds of ye Pattent ye sd 100 acres of land being
formerly granted to THO: IVEY by Pattent dated ye 22 Aug 1648 & THO: &
GEO: IVEY his sonnes since his decease sould unto WM: RICHARDSON and by
the sd RICHARDSON sould unto ye said THROWER And by these severall
seales (sales) will at large appeare in the Records of LNco in Jun 1673.
(Your editor can find no pattent in Nugent to THO: IVEY in 1648 or any
other date. Perhaps it will turn up in LNco Records. AGW) (see below)

23 Oct 1673 - ANTHONY LAWSON 490 acres in Lower Norfolk County at the
   (p473)   EASTERNE BRANCH of Elizabeth River in the woods neare
            BROAD CREEKE adjoyned Southward on the marked trees of
MR: WM: MOSELEYS land and the land of WM: HANCOCK and running from the
said HANCOCKS mkd trees along the mkd trees of MR: ffOWLERS land NE $\frac{1}{2}$ E
144 po then W by N 394 po then SSW 30 po then WNW 346 po so unto the
land of ROBERT YOUNG of BROAD CREEKE then SW by W 159 po to the land of
WM: MARTIN then E 180 po then S 114 po unto the mkd trees of MR: WM:
·MOSELEYS land. Due for trans: of 10 psons: Himselfe twice, JNO:
BAXTER, WM: CHURCH, GARRETT REALLY, ELIZ: MAY, WM: COOKE, EDWD: STANLEY,
Sambro & Marea, Negroes.

23 Oct 1673 - THOMAS VICESIMUS IVEY 620 acres in Lower Norfolk County
   (p473)   at the head of the EASTERNE BRANCH of Elizabeth River in
            the County of Lower Norfolk. 170 acres thereof being pt
of a Patt: of 200 acres formerly granted to COL: JNO: SIDNEY and by him
sould to GEO: KEMP and thence by severall assigmts: belongs unto ye sd
IVEY. The other 450 acres adjoyning being newly taken up and bounded
as followeth: lying in the woods betweene ye lands of the head of the
EASTERNE BRANCH aforesd: and the land of the head of SAMLL: BENNETTS
CREEK. Beginning at a corner tree of WM: HANCOCKS land thence running
by severall lines drawne first NNE 100 po then ESE 80 po then E by S $\frac{1}{2}$
S 80 po then NE by E $\frac{1}{2}$ E 246 po then S 192 po then W 56 po then S $\frac{1}{2}$ W
100 po then S by W $\frac{1}{2}$ W 10 po then W by N 310 po then N by W 86 po unto
the first station. 170 acres due as aforesaid & 450 acres being due
for trans: of 9 psons: THO: VICESIMUS IVEY, ALICE IVEY, MARY IVEY,
MARY EDEN, JNO: PAINE, WM: EDWARDS, GRACE DUNN, a Negroe & an Indian.
(See Nugent p 155 - John Sydney 200 acres upon Nwd side of E. br of
Eliz. Riv. 16 Sep 1644) (Note:- This Thomas Vicesimus Ivey is the son,
mentioned in the patent to Jno: Thrower at the top of this page, with
his brother George. AGW)

23 Oct 1673 - MORGAN MOORE 125 acres of land in Lower Norfolk County
   (p473)   on the SOUTH SIDE of the EASTERNE BRANCH of Elizabeth Riv-
            er beginning at a corner tree of RICH: KINGS standing by
the MAINE BRANCH side and running 320 po S into the woods and from
thence E 20 po joyning to the land of THO: WATKINS & from thence N 160
po to the head of a small branch from thence NE 160 po to the mouth of
a small creeke and then by ye River side W 100 po to the first station.
75 acres part thereof being part of a Patent of 150 acres formerly
granted to HEN: NICKLIS by him sould unto THO: WATKINS the said WATKINS

sould unto ye sd MOORE. Ye other 50 acres formerly granted to the sd
WATKINS by Patt: dated 5 Jul 1653 & sould to the sd MORGAN MOORE. (for
Tho: Watkins patent see Nugent p 239. No patent for Henry Nicklis
found in Nugent, however, there is one for Henry Nicholls 100 acs
22 Nov 1651 - no bounds are given)

23 Oct 1673 - WM: WATKINS 225 acres in Lower Norfolk County in ye
     (p474)   SOUTHERNE SIDE of the EASTERNE BRANCH of Elizabeth River
               75 acres part thereof being part of a Pattent of 150 acres
formerly granted HEN: NICKLIS and by several assigmts come unto THO:
WATKINS late decd & belonging to ye said WM: WATKINS as heire to ye said
THO: WATKINS and bounding according to the sale recorded in LNco will
appeare ye other 150 acres bounded on ye Northerne parts with ye abovesaid land and the land of MACHA? *matha* (Mathew? Mathias and Wm:
Whitehurst lived close together   in LNco) MATHIAS & WM:
WHITEHURST unto ye land of WM: ROGERS then along the said ROGERS marked
trees SSW 108 po thence WNW 204 po unto the land of DAVID MARRO *marro*
then N by E 78 po then WNW 48 po then NNE 28 po unto the aforesaid Devident of said WATKINS being due for trans: of 3 psons: JNO: DAVIS,
GRIFFIN GWYN, ROBT: DUNSCON? (or DUNSTON) *Dunston*

23 Oct 1673 - GEO: ffOWLER 550 acres in Lower Norfolk County in pish
     (p474)   of Linhaven at the head of CORNIX DAMS beging: at a red
               oake being a corner mkd tree of MOSLEYS (sic) land thence
by severall lines of mkd trees as followeth: First SSW 212 po then
W 15° Sly 96? po then SW 212? po then S by W 300 po then WNW 279 po to
a Quarter tree of WILL: HANCOCKS land then NE ½ E 384 po then NW 40°Wly
39 po then NE by N 350 po to the first station. 100 acres part thereof
being part of a Patt: of 750 acres formerly granted unto LT: COL: THO:
LAMBERT decd comonly called PUCKETTS NECKE (PUGGETTS NECK?) and sold
unto the sd ffowler by LEWIS BANDERMULL *Bandermull* (VANDERMULL is
his correct name AGW) as marying on(e)   of the co-heirs
of the said LAMBERT as by bill of sale dated ye 8 Mar 1669/70 will at
large appeare upon ye county records of LN the other 400 acres for
transportation of 8 psons: EDWD: ABBOTT, GRACE ARNOLD, ALICE ELLIS,
ANN STEGG, JNO: WELLS, HEN: SELBY and 2 Negroes. (See Nugent p 173
for Thomas Lambert patent 1 Jun 1648. Called PAGGETTS Neck, however
it is PUGGETTS NECK - see Nugent p 169 William Lucas 800 acres 22 Aug
1647 Beg. two points below the place where the Bay devides itself into
two branches, etc. Formerly granted unto CASAR HUGGETT (Puggett) 21
Dec 1643 and due sd Lucas by intermarriage with the relict & Admx. of
sd. Huggett and taken up by said Lucas as deserted land. See Nugent
p 150 - CESAR PUGGETT 800 acres 19 Dec 1643 On N side of KIRDY BRANCH)

23 Oct 1673 - JAMES WHITEHURST 400 acres in Lower Norfolk County at
     (p474)   the 3 Runns of the EASTERNE RIDGES. Beginning at a mkd
               tree by the Dams on WM: NICKLIS his land and bounded by
severall lines of mkd trees drawne as followeth. First NE 3/4 E 1X0
(100?) po then NW by W 100 po then NE by N 210 po then E by S 182 po
then S by W 278 po then W 280 po unto the first begining. Due for
trans: of 8 psons: 3 Negroes, ffRA: CHRISTOPHER, AMEY EDCARR? *Edcarr*
HEN: GARDNER, ROBT: BOWERS, PETER RIGLESWORTH.

23 Oct 1673 - WM: ELLIOT sonn of LT: COLL ANTHONY ELLIOT decd 340 acres
   (P475)   in Glouster County. Among the head rights is HENRY HERB-
               ERT.

25 Oct 1673 - NICHOLAS MILLECHOP 400 acres in Northampton County.....
   (p477)   land of JOHN PARKER.....former patent of 550 acres dated
               9 Oct 1672.

(Note:- There have been many patents for 23 Oct 1673 in Lower Norfolk
County. The patents from page 475 and 476 are Glocester County, page
477 is several patents in Northampton County with the last patent on
the page as follows:)

25 Oct 1673 - THO: GOODACRE 125 acres in Lower Norfolk County on SAMLL:
   (p477)   BENNETTS CREEKE and running from said creeke betweene the
               lands of ROWLAND MORGAN and THO: DAVIS by 2 parrellell
(sic) lines drawne NNW 323 po & runing for Bredth WSW 62 po & ½ the sd
land is part of a devident of 500 acres of land granted to JOHN LANG-
FIELD (spelled LANCKFIELD in some earlier records) by patt: dated 10
Feb 1637 and by ye sd LANGSTONE (sic) assigned to WILL: EAST and by sd
EAST inhis last will bequeathed to JOHN STRATON and by HEN: STRATON bro:
& heire of the sd JNO: STRATON the sd 125 acres sould to the sd THO:
GOODACRE.

25 Oct 1673 - JNO: AXTELL 400 acres of land in Lower Norfolk County to
   (p478)   ye SOUTHERD (sic) of ROODEE (RUDEE) beginning at a mkd
               white oake at the marsh side of the FRESH POND thence
running NE along the pond and alsoe W by N 376 po along the mkd trees
of WM: BROCKS land and to another devident of land belonging to the said
BROCK then NE by E ½ E 317 po then E by N 72 po then SE ½ E 186 po unto
the aforesd: NE line the said land was formerly granted to JNO: POORE
by Patt: dated 25 Feb 1664/5 and by the sd POORE assigned to RICHD:
BONNY 15 Nov 1665 and by the sd BONNY assigned the 15 Jun 1666 to the
sd JNO: AXTELL. (No patent in Nugent to JNO: POORE)

27 Oct 1673 - HEN: ffILMER 350 acres in WARWICK COUNTY according to
   (p481)   the Ancient & Lawfull bounds &c formerly granted unto
               ANTHONY BARNHAM decd and lately found to Escheate to his
Maties:.........&........now granted to sd HENRY ffILMER.

28 Oct 1673 - JOHN PORTER SENR: 3000 acres in Lower Norfolk County
   (p485)   in the woods adjoyning on WESTERNE SIDE of the RUNN of
               that ASHEN SWAMP which lyeth nere the Path which leadeth
from the EASTERNE BRANCH of ELIZABETH RIVER unto the NORTH RIVER and
bounded as followeth. Begin: at the Northeasterne Corner tree of the
aforesd: PORTERS 300 acres of land which (is?) part of his 350 acres
granted him by Patt: dated 16 Mar 1663/4 & from thence running S by E
320 po then W by S 176 po thence S by E unto the marked trees of the
land surveyed for JAMES WHITEHURST alsoe from the first beginning
running E ½ N 136 po unto the mkd corner tree of the land granted to
WM: EDWARDS thence S by E 321 po by the said EDWARDS his mkd trees &
then Downe that Runn unto a Cypress Swamp and then along the Western

side of that Cypress Swamp unto the marked trees of ffRA: SHIPP his land
at the foote of GODFREYS RUNN and then along the said SHIPS mkd trees
which are drawne S by W 248 po unto a Cypress Swamp and thence Runing
up the Easterne side of the Cypress Swamp unto the mkd trees of ye land
surveyed for JA: WHITEHUST (sic) and then along the said WHITEHUSTS mkd
trees unto <u>the of the former former bounds</u> (sic). Due for trans: of 60
persons: JOANE BURCH, ELIZ: STRATFORD, DANLL: COALSTONE, MICH: TRYTEN,
JANE JACOBE, ELIZ: CHAMBERLEN, HENRY CONER, JNO: JAWNER? (Joyner?), THO:
TUNNELL, ABIGALL SELLWOOD, Mingo a negroe, WM: DERIDGE, JNO: MOLLEENE,
ANN GOODBY twice, ROBT: BURGESS, RICH: BLEWETT, MARY OWEN, WM: PAINTER,
RICHD: HOLLAND, JNO: LAMPLAPH (or HAMPLAPH?), RICHD: TOLSON, MARY ATKINS,
THO: _unte?, EDW: STANLEY, JA: HEIG, THO: PITKIN (or PICKIN), Peter an
Indian, Rose, Doll, Mary, Besse, negroes, CHA: GRANDY, JO: STROUD, ANN
ffISHER, JNO: MEDEN (or NEDEN), PATRICK KYLE, ANN CLARKE, CHA: BELVIN,
JNO: PEARSE, CORN: MATHENNEY, THO: WINCK, SAMLL: PALMER, WM: BEVERLY,
HEN: BLUNDEN, OLIVER OZBORNE, ffRA TAYLOR, JA: COTTON, JNO: ROLE, ROBT:
CRUMPTON, JNO: FENTRIS, JA: EUDLING, JNO: LOW, RICH: HEW, HEN: BARTON,
THO: STOUT, THO: WAUKLING, WILL: RUB?, MARY PETTHOUSE.

29 Oct 1673 - RICHD: WILLIAMS 176 acres 1/2 of land in Lower Norfolk
   (p485)   County in DANLL: TANNERS CREEKE begining at a mkd Red
               Oake thence running downe the Creeke NE 200 po to the
head of a branch of the LITTLE CREEK thence NW 134 po to a mkd oake soe
SW alongst the land of JNO: OZBORNE 100 po to a mkd white oake thence
SE 134 po to the first station. Due for trans: of 4 psons: No names
given.   (Note: I think this means 176½ acres of land AGW)

3 Oct 1673 - THOMAS MERSER (MERCER) 200 acres in Lower Norfolk County
   (p488)   in a Creeke called PUSELL (PUZZLE) POYNT CREEKE being a
               branch of the SOUTHERNE BRANCH of Elizabeth River begin:
at a mkd white oake standing at the Creeke side on ye South side of the
Creeke & soe running for breadth SSE 100 po to a mkd pine and soe for
length WSW 320 po to a mkd Beach and soe againe for breadth NNW 100 po
by certaine mkd trees to the Creeke side & soe downe the Creekside ENE
320 po to ye first menconed mkd tree. The sd land being formerly
granted unto RICHARD STARNELL & since sould by MICH: WAYBOURNE to ye
sd THO: MERSER. (Nugent p 255 - Richard Starnell 200 acs 20 Apr 1653.
No bounds given and this is the only patent in Nugent which could have
been in the Southern Branch.)

4 Nov 1673 - JOHN GAMMON 500 acres in Lower Norfolk County begin: at
   (p489)   a certaine mkd beech neare the parting of the 2 Swamps the
               one called RIDGFORD, the other CYPRES SWAMP and runing up
by or neare the sd CYPRES SWAMP SW ½ W 455 po to another mkd beech th:
ESE 340 po to a mkd oake th: Downe the said RIDGFORD SWAMP to the first
station. Due for the trans: of 10 psons: JAMES GAMERELL, MARY CREED,
JONE JENNINGS, PRES: DORRINGTON, MARY COOPER, MATH: ALBOTS, JNO: LOW,
ELINOR NASH, LAZRUS JENKINS, HERD TAYLOR.

5 Nov 1673 - JNO: BOWSEY 1668 acres of land in Rappahannock County.
   (p492)   Head rights include: JONAS TURNER & SUSAN TURNER.

6 Nov 1673 - ROBERT HODGES   280 acres in Lower Norfolk County being in
   (p494)   LINHAVEN on the WEST SIDE of SAMLL: BENNETTS CREEKE at
                the head of the CATTAYLE BRANCH, thence runs first NNW 46
po th: WSW 250 po then SSE 162 po th: NW 232 po then ENE 350 po then
SSE 178 po unto the head of a branch then downe the SW side of that br:
and up the NE side of another branch unto the head thereof and the
first station. Sd 280 acres being due as followeth 250 acres pte thereof formerly granted to SAVILL GASKINS by patt: dated 20 Oct 1661 and
sold unto WILLIAM HODGE as by assignmt of the said Patt: as will appeare
in Lower Norfolk records 29 Oct 1662. The other 30 acres being pte of
a parcell of land of one LANCFIELDS patt: sould unto the sd WILLIAM
HODGE and now the whole 280 acres being due to ROBERT HODGE as heire
to his brother WILLIAM HODGE late deseased. (See Nugent pp 269, 415
Savill Gaskin).

8 Nov 1673 - CAPT: JOHN SAVAGE 900 acres in Northampton County former-
   (p495)   ly granted to HANNAH SAVEDGE (sic) 24 Aug 1635 & renewed
                in CAPT: JOHN SAVEGES name 28 Nov 1664. A former pattent
of COL: JOHN STRINGER & ANNE his wife in 1663 is menconed as being due
to CAPT: JOHN SAVAGE.

18 Feb 1673/4-WM: HERNDON   180 acres in New Kent County. Among the
   (p502)   head rights are: GEO: TURNER & GEO: RIDLEY.

2 Mar 1673/4- THO: PIERCE   155 acres in WARWICK COUNTY and MULBERY IS-
   (p506)   LAND PISH bounded.......a point neare WARWICK RIVER side
                ......along Warwick River.......mkd oak in GEO: HARWOODS
line neare sd HARWOODS house.....for trans: of 3 psons: WM: ffOARD
(Ford?), JOSEPH HABERD (or HUBERD), JNO: MILLS.

8 Apr 1674 - RICHD: WHITEHEAD 2000 acres in New Kent County. Among
   (p508)   the head rights are listed: JNO: WILKINSON, THO: WRIGHT
                and SARAH MARSH.

21 Sep 1674 - GEO: PEARCE 2100 acres in Nansemond County. Among the
   (p519)   head rights: THO: TURNER.

21 Sep 1674 - GYLES DRIVER   930 acres of land in Isle of Wight part of
   (p520)   sd land formerly granted sd Gyles dated 26 8ber 1662.

23 Sep 1674 - WM: HAVEROMB 905 acres in Lower Norfolk County on the
   (p526)   SOUTH SIDE of the EASTERNE BRANCH of Elizabeth River near
                the Head of it and begin: att MR: JNO PORTER SEGR: his
corner mkd tree being an ash in the ASHEN SWAMP from thence runing 30
po by E to a mkd white oak standing nere the Ashen Swamp runs soe by
the side of the sd run severall Southerly Courses to a mkd oak from th:
80 po SE by S to JAMES JOSLINGS corner mkd tree being a gum and by the
sd JOSLINGS line of mkd trees NNE 250 po & continueing the sd NNE line
70 po further to another mkd Gum. Then N 120 po to another mkd tree
att the head of the LITTLE CYPRESS BRANCH from th: againe N 690 po a-
long the side of a thick Reedy Pocoson to a mkd beech standing nigh
JAMES & JNO: KEMPS lyne of mkd trees then by the sd KEMPS line 200 po

W by N then N by W 8 po to ISAACK HOCKERS land & from th: by the sd
HOCKERS land 200 po W by S to the first station. Sd land being due to
sd HAVERCOMB? by & for trans: of 18 psons: JNO: COSTI? JNR:, 2 Indians,
Jone a negro, MARY ROBINSON, ELIZA: CAYNE?, GABRIELL JACOB, RICH: WAL-
POOLE, LEAGE (or Wage?) ADALE, GEORGE JACK?, JNO: ALFORD, JNO: MARSHALL,
MARY CANTON, JNO: BROADAR, JNO: HILLERY, SAM: ARACING, OWEN LEWIS, JNO:
-faded -.

23 Sep 1674 - JAMES HANDSON 158 acres in Lower Norfolk County att the
   (p526)   Head of the INDIAN CREEK in Elizabeth River beginning at
               a mkd read oak standing neere a branch of that creek and
soe from thence runing W 79 po to a long mkd pine standing in FADING
SWAMP and from the sd pine S by E 320 po to a mkd white gum in another
Swamp & from thence East 79 po through the sd swamp to a mkd popler
thence by West 320 po allong the mkd trees of WM: & RICHARD WHITEHURST
& HENRY HOLSTEADS to the first mentioned mkd tree which standeth up in
that line. Due as followeth vizt: 100 acres thereof for trans: of 2
persons & 58 acres the residue formerly granted to the sd HOLSTEAD by
patt: dated 14 Sep 1667. MATHEW WILSON & WM: WILSON.
(Note:
        At beginning of above patent name is written:
        At end "58 acres the residue formerly granted
to sd. HOLSTEAD" see this patent on p 6 & 6 PB221.   )

26 7ber 1674- THOMAS GRIFFIN 250 acres of land in Lower Norfolk Coun-
   (p528)   ty called SURREY PLANTATION running for length NNE 421
              po alongst a marsh by a Creek runing Northerly out of
CURRATUCK BAY & from a corner of that Marsh alongst ye sd Creeke NNW
76 po for breadth to a corner pine thence SSW by a Swampside 421 po to
a corner pine thence ESE 76 po to ye first station Including alsoe a
small ISLAND called PINEY ISLAND lying Northerly from this land over
the sd Creek being due unto the sd THOMAS GRIFFIN by and for trans: of
5 persons: JNO ASHWORTH, himselfe & 3 negroes, MORRIS FITZGARRALL.

26 Sep 1674 - HUGH ffORGISON (FERGUSON?) 69 acres in Lower Norfolk Co.
   (p528)   begin: at a corner pine butting on the FRESH PONDS & soe
              runing W 21 po to a corner gum thence SSW ½ a point Wly
346 po to a corner maple thence SE 40 po to the head of ye DAMS th:
NNE ½ a point Ely 366 po alongst ye ponds side to ye first station.
The sd land being due for trans: of 2 psons: JNO: BUTTLER & DANIEL
AKERON.

26 7br 1674 - JOHN WHITE 195 acres in Lower Norfolk County in the
   (p528)   NORTHERNE BRANCH of CURRATUCK beginning at a Corner pine
              by a Marsh dividing MR. BASNETTS land & this & runing S
by W 150 po to a corner gum thence ESE 186 po to a corner pine thence
NNE 148 po by a line of mkd trees to a corner pine (on the?) Marsh side
that divides this land & THOMAS PITTS thence alongst the Creeke 250 po
to the first station WNW. Due for trans: of 4 psons: JNO: WHITE,
SUSAN WHITE, JNO: WHITE JUNR:, SOLOMON WHITE.

32

26 Sep 1674 - PETER MALBONE 250 acres in Lower Norfolk County called
   (p528)   by the name of LONG ISLAND bounded Eastward on the South-
               ward side & westward on CURRATUCK BAY including alsoe a
small island on the SEABORD SIDE Ely from LONG ISLAND. Sd land being
due for trans: of 5 psons; PETER MALBONE, MARGERY WARD, ELIZABETH
THOMPSON, JAMES HOGG, JNO: MILES.

26 7ber 1674- ROBT: SYMONDS (also SYMMOND) 74 acres in Lower Norfolk
   (p529)   County called by the name of CEDAR ISLAND lying Southerly
               from LONG ISLAND & bounded Eastward on the SEABORD SIDE &
westward on CURRATUCK BAY. Due for trans: of 2 psons: EDWARD PRICE,
TASSELL SHAW.

25 Sep 1674 - JOHN KEMP 500 acres in Lower Norfolk County in PISH of
   (p530)   LINHAVEN in the woods Northward from the EASTERNE BRANCH
               of Elizabeth River bounding Westward by the mkd trees of
the land granted to WM: EDWARDS and beg: 7 po to the Southward of the
sd EDWARDS his Southerne corner tree and thence bounded by severall
lines of mkd trees as followeth: first by S 302 po then NE ½ Ely 160
po then NW ½ W 236 po then W by N 288 po unto the land of the sd ED-
WARDS then S ½ (E?) 225 po unto the first beginning. Due for trans:
of 10 persons: ARTHUR TOPPIN himselfe 5 times & his wife once,
ISAAC HOCKER MARY his wife, SUSANNA HOCKER, MICH: CLARE. (Arthur
Toppin was decd in Dec 1671. His will is in Book E f 106 LNco Records)

28 Sep 1674 - MICHAEL MACOY 150 acres in Lower Norfolk County in the
   (p530)   Parish of Linhaven in the head of the lands on the SOUTH
               SIDE of the EASTERNE BRANCH of Elizabeth River begin: on
the land of DAVID MURROW th: runing by severall lines of mkd trees as
first ESE 204 po th: S by W ½ W 124 po th: W ½ N 140 po unto the land
of DAVID MURROW th: along the sd MURROWES mkd trees Northerly unto his
first begining. Due for trans: of 3 persons: WILLIAM LAMPERT, EDWARD
DAVIS, RACHELL WETHERLY.

28 Sep 1674 - THO: BOWLER 504 acres in Rappahannock County. Land of
   (531)   JAMES BAGNALL decd adjacent to this patent.

29 Sep 1674 - CORNELIUS ELLIS 82 acres of land in Lower Norfolk County
   (p532)   on the EASTERN SIDE of the SOUTHERNE BRANCH of Elizabeth
               River begin: at a mkd white oake standing neer the head
of a small Creeke running from thence W 73 po along WIRGROVES? land to
another mkd white oak from thence S 40 po to a small mkd pine in a
poynt at ye head of a Gutt & thence NW ½ N 90 po by ye sd Gutts side
to a mkd Pine on the mouth thereof from thence N 80 po then 50 po NE
to a mkd pine at ye mouth of the aforesd Creek soe up the Creek to ye
first station. Due for trans: of 2 psons: JOHN ADDAMS, TYMOTHY HARRA?

21 Sep 1674 - THO: ffENFORD 300 acres in Lower Norfolk County begin:
   (p545)   at a corner tree of a former patt: of his and at the miles
               end & soe running 320 po SW to a white oke (sic) & from
th: 150 po NW and from thence NE 320 po & from thence SE joyning his
owne land 150 po to the first station. For Trans: of 6 psons: THO:

CULSON, JNO: MORFIELD, JNO: BRAY, WM: MORGAN, JNO: ROBARDSON, BARTHO:
BEE.

29 Nov 1674 - JAMES HARRISON, JOHN BOWZEE, & ELIZ:, MARGERETT, ANN &
   (p546)   ELIN MOTT, orphans of MR. GEO: MOTT - 9019 acres on the
            South side of Rappahannock River. PETER RIDLEY & WM:
WEST two of the 180 head rights.

26 Jan 1674/5- JNO: WILLIAMSON JR: 758 acres in Lower Norfolk County
   (p553)   in TANNERS CREEKE PRECINCT begin: at a Corner Pine stand-
           ing neere the head of the fresh runn Branch & runing W
$\frac{1}{2}$ Nly 75 po to a corner red oake at the head of LAZARUS JENKINGS land
then S $\frac{1}{2}$ Ely 64 po to a corner red oake in RICHARD JONES line then SE
40 po alongst his line to a corner red oake then SSE 14 po alongst this
line to a corner Pine thence SE by S 300 po alongst his line 88 po to a
Corner Maple in a Swamp th: S $\frac{1}{2}$ Wly 60 po alongst his line to a corner
white oake th: E by N 226 po by a line of mkd trees to a corner gum by
a branch side betweene the BLACK WALNUTT NECK and the LONG NECK th: NE
60 po alongst a Small Creeke to a corner pine then E $\frac{1}{2}$ Nly 36 po to a
corner white oake on GATERS CREEK side thence N 1/4 Wly alongst a
small Creeke to a corner Pine th: NNE 54 po to a corner Red Oake on the
same Creeke th: NW $\frac{1}{2}$ Nly 40 po to a corner Pine on the same Creeke th:
N $\frac{1}{2}$ Wly 60 po to a corner pine on the same Creeke th: NNW $\frac{1}{2}$ Wly 24 po
to a corner Pine at the mouth of the same Creeke thence NW by W $\frac{1}{2}$ Wly
168 po alongst TANNERS CREEKE to a corner Pine th: NNE 16 po to a
corner Locust on the same Creeke th: WNW $\frac{1}{2}$ Wly 20 po to a corner Pine
of the same creeke th: W $\frac{1}{2}$ Sly 44 po to a corner Pine at the Mouth of
the FRESH RUNN CREEKE th: SW by W $\frac{1}{2}$ Wly 110 po up ye sd Creeke to a
corner Pine th: S $\frac{1}{2}$ point Wly 60 po to a corner Pine th: W $\frac{1}{2}$ point Sly
92 po to the first station. 644$\frac{1}{2}$ acres of sd land formerly granted
WILLIAMSON by Pat 16 Mar 1655 the other the 24 Aug 1660, the remainder
113 acres due for trans: of 3 psons: DANLL: NEGLETIME?, JNO: PIERCE?,
MARY WILLIAMS(ON?). (The names are faded. Williams is the way Mary's
name is written, however, Williamson is in the Norfolk records as
Williams many times. AGW)

10 Jun 1675 - JNO: ADAMS 160 acres in Lower Norfolk County on the
   (p555)   NORTH SIDE of ELIZABETH RIVER beg: at a small Poynt and
           runing by the Creeke side E 160 po joyning to the S side
of his former land & soe away S by his line of trees 100 po to a marked
white oak from thence W 160 po to the head of a small creeke th: N 160
po to the first station. For trans: of 3 persons. (Names not given)

15 Jun 1675 - PHILIP LIGHTFOOT 150 acres in Gloster County. Land of
   (p557)   JNO: BANISTER mentioned. (One side of this patent is
           badly faded.

4 Oct 1675 - HENRY BUTT 320 acres in Lower Norfolk County being on
   (p564)   the Easterne side of ROBT: BUTTS land begin: at a mkd
           white oake standing nigh to a mkd -(blank)- of ROBT:
BUTTS & runing E? by S 160 Po to a marked pine th: S by W 300 po to a

mkd white oake th: W by S 100 po to a mkd pine bounding on ROBERT BUTTS
mkd trees & soe NW 100 po & then N by E bounding on the said BUTTS line
240 po to the first station. Sd land was formerly granted to ANTHONY
BENFORD by patt: dated 6 Nov 1665 and for want of seateing was by him
deserted and...16 Jun 1675 was granted to the sd BUTT & is parte due
by transportation of 7 psons: THO: CALSON (CARLSON?), JNO: BRAY, WM:
MORGAN, JNO: RICHARDSON, JNO: MORFEILD, BUTT BECA?, EDW: JAMES

9 Oct 1675 - EDWARD OWLD (OLD) 452 acres in Lower Norfolk County in
   (p570)   the LOWER PARISH of LINHAVEN begin: at a pine on the bot-
               tom of a point of ye MIDDLE NECK dividing two small
creeks & running over one of ye Creeks to BRUSHY NECK NW by W ½ Wly 96
po to a corner pine on xxxx a Creek side then W by N ½ N by lyne sd
trees (sic) 320 po to a corner Beech by a CYPRESS SWAMP th: S by W 40
po to a corner gum by the sd swamp side th: E 30 po to a white oake th:
S by E 280 po to a gum by the horse path th: SE by E ½ E bounding on
MR: BASNETT 118 po to a red oak at ye head of a branch th: NE 298 po
bounding on a Creeke to the first station. Due for trans: of 9 psons:
a negro boy called Jack, a negro woman called Jane, THO: SAMPSON, JNO:
HEWES (HUGHES?), JOHN DAVID, JOHN CABIDGE, EDWD STENTON, RICHARD KNIGHT,
PHILIP WILLIAMS.

9 Oct 1675 - THOMAS BENSON 100 acres in Lower Norfolk County in the
   (p580)   PARISH of LYNHAVEN begin at a corner gum by a CYPRES
               SWAMP & runing S 50 po to a holy (holly) th: SW 28 po to a
hicory th: SW by S 165 po to a white oak in a POQUOSON th: NW by W 66
po to a pine in a Poquoson th: NNE 104 po to a gum in a Poquoson th:
ENE 65 po to a holy th: N by W 30 po to a gum th: NE 30 po to a gum in
the CYPRES SWAMP th: bounding on the sd Swamp E 1/4 Sly 50 po to the
first station. For trans: of two persons: ALICE MORTON & JOHN UBLE.

9 Oct 1675 - JOHN VAUGHAN 221 acres in Lower Norfolk County on the
   (p580)   SOUTH SIDE of BLACK WATER CREEKE begin: at a corner pop-
               lar standing by a Poquoson side & running NW by W ½ Wly
34 po to a red oak by ye creeke side th: W ¼ Nly 49 po alongst the
Creek to a white oake by a marsh side th: WSW ½ Sly 56 po to a beech by
the the Creeke side th: S by W ½ Wly 84 po to a pine th: SW 102 po to a
pine by a Reedy Swamp th: SE ¼ Sly 102 po to a pine th: E ½ Nly 40 po
to a holy bush th: ESE 34 po to a red oake th: NE ½ Ely 45 po to a gum
by a branch side th: N ½ Ely 36 po alongst the sd branch to a pine by
a poquoson side th: bounding on the sd poquoson N by E ¼ Ely 188 po to
the first station. For trans: of 5 psons: JNO: VAUGHAN, WM: CONNER,
CHARLES CORNELIUS, JAMES SMOTHER, ELIZABETH RUFF (or Russ or Rust?)

9 Oct 1675 - THOMAS TOOLEY 150 acres in Lower Norfolk County on the
   (p580)   NORTH SIDE of BLACK WATER CREEK beginning at a corner pine
               neare the said creek & runing N by W 139 po by mkd trees
to a Corner Maple th: W by S 173 po by mkd trees to a pine th: S by E
139 po towards the creeke th: East by N bounding on the sd creeke 173
po to the first station. The sd land being due by and for the trans:
of three persons: THO: TOOLEY & his wife, THO: TOOLEY.

9 Oct 1675 - WM: CORNICKS 238 acres in Lower Norfolk County in the
   (p580)   Parish of Lynhaven begin: at a corner red oake standing
               on CHINCOPIN RIDGE in his old line & running SW by S
162 po to a holy (holly) by the BUSHY RIDGE th: S ½ Ely 108 po to a
beech th: W by N 62 po to a poplar th: N ½ Wly 108 po to a beech th:
W by S 100 po to a beech th: NNW 32 po to a beech on the POPLAR RIDGE
th: W 26 po to a Poplar th: N ½ Wly 100 po to a holy th: NE by E 60 po
to a beech th: ESE 176 po to a beech by the path side th: NE by N 116
po to a red oake in his old line th: S by E 59 po alongst his old line
to the first station for transportation of 5 persons: AN HARRIS, MARY
HILL, JDITH WARNER, ELIZAB: DAVID, MARGARET JONES.

9 Oct 1675 - JOHN GRIFFIN 179 acres in Lower Norfolk County of land
   (p580)   named GRIFFINS POINTS lying on the EAST SIDE of ye NORTH
RIVER begin: at a Corner red oake butting on a dams (sic) & runing W 78
po bounding on COLLO: MASON & MR. ffOWLERS line to a red oake th: N 1/4
Ely bounding on the sd MASONS & FOWLERS line 142? po (could be 242 or
even 442 the way it is written) to a pine in a poquoson th: W by S ½
Sly 97 po to a gum th: SSE 9 po to a maple th: SW by W 88 po to a pine
on a marsh th: S 1/4 Wly 40 po to a gum on the River th: ESE 70 po to a
pine on the river th: S 1/4 Wly 96 po to a pine on the river th: SE 26
po to a pine on a marsh th: bounding on the sd marsh NE ½ Ely 200 po to
the first station. For trans: of 5 persons: THOMAS OWENS, THOMAS HILL,
JNO: PEAD, HANNAH SNEAD.

9 Oct 1675 - HENRY WOODHOUSE 441 acres in Lower Norfolk County beeing
   (p581)   part of ye LONG RIDGE Southerly from RICHARD BONNIES line
               beginning at a corner holy in a poquoson neare BONNIES
line and runing alongst his line E by S 140 po to a red oak th: S 142
po through a poquoson to a gum th: WNW 33 po to a pine thence S by W
82 po to a white oake th: SE 44 po to a maple th: Sby W 161 po to a
pine th: W by N 120 po (looks like 920) to a maple th: SSW ½ Wly 62 po
to a red oake th: NW by W 156 po to a pine th: N by E 398 po to the first
station for trans: of 9 persons: DANIEL ANDERSON, EDWARD OULDS, URSLA
THORNTON, EDWARD STRINGER, CHARLES HENDLEY, ROBERT RICHMOND, PATRICK
ANGUIS, two negroes Roger & Bess.

9 Oct 1675 - ROBT: SYMONDS 100 acres of land in Lower Norfolk County
   (p581)   called THE GOOD LAND begin: at a Corner Pine butting on a
               Marsh on CURRETUCK BAY & running alongst the Marsh side
S ½ p⁰ Ely 266 po to a corner pine on the same Marsh th: NNW into the
woods 60 po th: N ½ a point Wly 266 po to a stake in a small gutt in a
Marsh th: along the sd Marsh side ESE 60 po to the first station. For
trans: of two persons: THO: PITTS & JNO: BECK.

9 Oct 1675 - WILLIAM LANGLEY 829 acres 3 rood & 14 po of land lying
   (p581)   in TANNERS CREEK in Lower Norfolk County begin: at a cor-
               ner pine on a POINT of ye MAINE CREEKE & running NNE 140
po to HORNERS GUTT th: N by W 80 po to the mouth of CRAB POINT CREEK th:
NE ½ Nly alongst the sd Creeke 160 po to a corner pine th: alonge the
sd creeke E by N 126 po to a pine th: NNE 34 po to a white oake th: S
by E 22 po to a red oake th: SSW 92 po by mk'd trees to a Cedar by a

Creeke side th: along the Creek SW 40 po to a pine th: S 64 po alongst
the sd Creek to a white oake th: SE by mkd trees 48 po to a red oake th:
S ½ Ely 24 po to a pine th: W 36 po to a corner cedar th: SSW 90 po by
a line of marked trees to a corner pine th: W by N 74 po to a Corner
pine th: SSE 40 po to a corner pine on a Creek th: SSW 100 po alongst
the sd creek to a corner pine th: SW ½ Wly alongst the sd Creek 86 po
to a corner White oake on the Creeke th: alongst the sd creeke NW by W
280 po to the first station. 200 acres of which land was formerly granted unto the sd WM: LANGLEY by patt: bearing date 21 9ber <u>1625</u> & 629 acres
3 rood & 14 po of land being due unto ye sd LANGLEY for trans of 13 persons: ANDREW WHITE, WM: HADLEY, JNO: KING, THO: ATKINS, MICHAEL WADE,
PHILIP BROWNE, THO: HARDING, WM: ROSS, HUGH JONES & 3 negroes, ROBT:
BROOKS. (Note: The 1625 date is no mistake it is so written in the patent. There is a patent to WM: LANSDEN of KIQUOTAN in the Corporation of
Elizabeth City, yeoman, "an old planter"...for his first psonnel Devident........100 acres on the Northerne side of Southampton River. The
name is clearly written Lansden, however, I have wondered if it might
not be Wm: Langley of Lower Norfolk, which county was settled at a later
date ca. 1635. The 1625 patent is apparently non-existant at this date.
(see Nu 6 & 1 PB pt 1 p 41) AGW)

9 Oct 1675 - WM: WEST 656 acres in Lower Norfolk County on the East
   (p582)   side of the NORTH RIVER 400 acres of which land was form-
                 erly granted unto the sd WEST by pattent dated 27 May
1673 & 256 acres bounded vizt: begin: at a corner maple by a poquoson
of the river & runing E by N 92 po to a corner pine th: NE 82 po to a
corner Holy thence E 60 po to a corner pine in his old line th: SW 68 po
th: S 126 po th: SSE 96 po to a corner white oak in his old line th:
SE by E 31 po to a corner gum th: SW by W 42 po to a corner gum th: WNW
½ Wly 214 po to the river th: N ½ Ely 164 po bounding on the river and
the Poquoson of the river to the first station for the trans: of 5 persons: WM: WEST, WM: WEST (sic), LAWRENCE BOUCHER, RICHARD HANDICK,
HENRY SOUTHERNE.

9 Oct 1675 - JOHN ADAMS 170 acres in Lower Norfolk County lying in
   (p582)   ELIZABETH RIVER PARISH beginning at a point between 2
                 small Creeks in ELLETS CREEK & running NE ½ Ely 28 po th:
ENE ½ Ely 140 po alongst the sd Creek to a corner Bla: gum by a gutt
side th: SE by S 100 po by mkd trees to a corner white oake th: S ½ Wly
30 po to a corner white oake by the roadside th: E by S 46 po to a Corner Cedar by a branch side th: SE by S 23 po to a corner pine by a
creekside th: SW ½ Wly 92 po to a corner holy by a branch side th: a-
long the sd Branch NNW 18 po to a corner Dogwood th: W by N 111 po by
a line of mkd trees to a corner pine th: NW by N 94 po bounding on the
GLEBE LAND to ye mouth of a small gutt th: WNW 34 po to the first station. For trans: of 4 persons: JOHN CLEARE, ANDREW MARTIN, SAMUEL
GREEN, ELIZAB: RICHARDS.

9 Oct 1675 - ROBT: HARPER 220 acres 1 rood & 24 po in Parish of Lyn-
   (p582)   haven in Lower Norfolk County towards the head of
                 LYNHAVEN RIVER on the WESTERN SIDE called the AISHIN (Ash-
en? for Ash trees?) SWAMP begin: at a corner white oak on the head line

of RENATUS LAND his land & runing upon his line of mkd trees SE 248 po
to a corner stooping white oake th: S by W 173 po by a line of mkd
trees to a corner AISH by a Swamp side th: West 40 po to a corner beech
th: SSW 16 po to a corner beech th: WNW 53 po to a corner Maple by a
Swamp side th: N ½ Wly 340 po to the first station for trans of 5 persons: GILES COLLINS, EDWARD ROGERS, PETER MILLETT, LIDIA ALLEN,
CHRISTOPHER ALLEN.

9 Oct 1675 - MR: WM: NEWMAN   184 acres in Lower Norfolk County lying
   (p582)   in TANNERS CREEK precinct begin: at a Spanish Oake of
                ABRAH: ELLETS & running NW ly bounding on the sd ELLETT
320 po to a corner white oake th: SW by S 173 po bounding on the sd
ELLETT to a corner red oake in RICHARD JONES line th: alongst JONES his
line N ½ Ely 138 po to a corner white oake of JOHN WILLIAMSONS in the
same line th: along WILLIAMSONS line E by N 164 po to a corner pine in
the same line th: SSE 240 po by a line of mkd trees to a corner pine
in a Swamp th: ESE 60 po by a line of mkd trees to a corner gum th:
S ½ Wly 108 po to the first station. For transportation of 5 persons:
WM: PALMER, THOMAS DRAPER, WM: CORDRIDGE, THO: HEWES (HUGHES?).

9 Oct 1675 - WM: BASNETT   1150 acres in Lower Norfolk County in the
   (p583)   NORTHERN BRANCH of CURRETUCK BAY called by the name of
                COLCHESTER begin: at GEORGE INDIAN QUARTER & runing SW
by S 170 po alongst a marsh dividing JOHN WHITES land & this to a
corner pine th: W by S 100 po to a corner white oake th: NW 36 po to a
small Bla: gum th: NE by N alongst a marsh dividing GEORGE INDIAN QUAR-
TER & DANCING RIDGE 168 po to a corner white oake th: NE by E intersecting a small creek 90 po to a corner upon FRANK INDIAN QUARTER th:
NW by W 50 po to a corner Sweet gum th: NNE ½ Ely 357 po to a corner
pine towards the head of the dams th: NW 41 po to a corner sweet gum
th: NE 60 po to a corner Red oake th: E 25 po to a corner gum upon the
GREEN BRANCH then alongst the sd branch S by E 212 po to a corner pine
on the Marsh side th: SW by S 160 po to a corner pine on the Marsh side
th: SSW 118 po to a point on the mouth of sd creek th: along the Creek
WNW 254 po to a small point opposite the first station th: SW by S 138
po intersecting a small creek to the first station. Including alsoe a
small ridge of land Easterly from this land & binding this land &
THOMAS GRIFFIN.   510 acres of which land was formerly granted unto sd.
BASNETT by patt: dated 10 7br 1664 & 640 acres being due for trans: of
13 persons: JNO: MORRIS, JNO: WRIGHT, JAMES SKERRER, DAVID ffREEMAN,
RICHARD JONES, SARAH WILLOUGHBY, ROBT: DARBY, JNO: BOULTON, JNO: SCOTT,
THO: JONES, ROBT: NOWELL, ARTHUR MAQUIN, ELIZABETH TWIST.

9 Oct 1675 - CAPT: WM: CARVER   784 acres in Lower Norfolk County in ye
   (p583)   parish of Lynhaven called by the name of BRINSONS QUARTER
                begin: at a corner Sweet Gum by the BROAD RIDGE RUN & soe
runing W by S 40 po to a corner maple th: SSW 6 po to a gum th: SW by
W ½ Wly 120 po th: SE 6 po th: SW by W 20 po to a corner beech th: E by
S ½ Ely 12 po to a corner beech th: S ½ Wly 66 po to a corner beech Th:
ESE 56 po to a corner beech th: S 50 po to a pine th: SE by E 36 po to
a holy th: S by W 58 po to a holy th: NW 20 po to a poplar th: SW by W
240 po to a beech & holy th: SE 70 po to a holy th: SW 36 po to a beech

th: SE by S 60 po th: S 34 po to a holy Th: SE 38 po to a pine Th: S 20
po to a beech th: ESE 20 po to a holy th: S 30 po to a beech th: ESE 24
po to a beech th: S 22 po to a holy th: SE 22 po to a beech th: East 24
po to a white oake th: SE by E 100 po by the PINEY SWAMP to a gum th:
NE 24 po to a maple th: N by E 22 po th: NNW 60 po to a gum th: NNE ½
Ely 90 po to a white oake th: N by W 84? (94?) po to a beech th: NNE
½Ely to a corner white oake on the edge of ye REEDY SWAMP 100 po th: N
420 po to the first station. For trans: of 16 persons: JNO: DATTED?,
MARY CARNETT, NORA BRIANT, RICH: HUDSON, BENJA: PICKWORTH, WM: BEVERLEY,
& his wife, JONE GETTEREY, CHRISTIAN BRUCE?, EDW: HOLLOWAY, CLEMT: HAR-
RISON, ELIZA: BARTON, THO: WAKEFIELD, AN SOMMERHILL, JAMES HARRALD?

9 Oct 1675   - JOHN KEELING 537 acres in Lower Norfolk County in the
   (p583/4)   parish of Lynhaven begin: at a corner white oak in his
               old survey & runing SE 320 po by mkd trees to a corner
maple in a Pocoson th: N by E by mkd trees 131 po to a corner gum th:
East 60 po to a corner Black gum th: N by E 176 po by mkd trees to a
corner gum on a Branch neare THOROWGOOD KEELINGS Land th: NNW bounding
on ye sd KEELINGS 62 po th: w 160 po bounding on the land of LT: THO:
KEELING decd. to ye road path by a REEDY BRANCH th: along the sd
branch WNW 110 po to a branch runing into LYNHAVEN RIVER th: bounding on the River SW by S 170 po to a Marsh neare the BRIDGE th: SE
44 po to the first station. 150 acres of which land was formerly
granted unto sd KEELING by patt: dated 9 Oct 1665 & 387 acres being
due for the trans: of 8 persons: GEORGE MINCHIN, SUSAN his wife,
RICHARD PARSONS, WM: GARRETT, HENRY BARNARD, CHARLES MICLERS?, JAMES
SNOWD (or SNOWE?), MATHEW DENNIS.

9 Oct 1675 - EDMUND MOORE 400 acres in Lower Norfolk County beginning
   (p584)   at a Corner Beech butting on a reedy & the NEGRO SWAMP &
               running SE 320 po to a corner beech th: S 46 po to a map-
le thence SW by W 120 po along the sd swamp to a Sassafras th: SSE 120
po to a beech on MARKED POPLAR RUN th: ENE 60 po to a holy on the PONDY
SWAMP th: along the sd swamp N by E 1/4 Ely 50 po to a hicory th: N by W
40 po to a Sorrell th: NNE 1/4 Ely 220 po by a piney & reedy swamp to a
holy bounding on the Cyprus Swamp th: N by W 66 po to a holy on the same
swamp th: SW 26 po to a pine th: NNW 100 po to a holy th: N by W 34 po
to a beech thence NW 22 po to a beech th: N 20 po to a maple th: W 26 po
to a white oake th: w 1/3 Sly 170 po to the first station. Including
alsoe a small ridge of land lying Southerly from the ENE line & neare
unto this land. For trans: of 8 persons: ffRANCIS DUN, MARGARET MOTLEY,
THO: EVANS, JAMES SHEPHERD, NICHOLAS DUGRAS, JNO: GUYDON, BENEDICT LEWIS.

9 Oct 1675 - LEMUEL MASON & MR. GEORGE ffOWLER 670 acres in Lower Nor-
   (p584)   folk County called by the name of MATCHEPONGO lying East-
               erly from ye NORTH RIVER begin: at a corner gum standing
in a Swamp neare the head of a Dam & runing SW by S alongst the dams
100 po to a corner red oake on the dams side thence W 78 po to a corner
red oake   N 1/4 Ely 142 po to a corner pine in a pocoson th: NE ½ Ely
90 po to a corner gum th: NNE 1/4 Ely 140 po to a corner red oake by a
pocosons side th: NW ½ Wly 60 po to a corner red oake th: SW ½ Wly 60 po
to a corner white oake th: NW ½ Wly 128 po alongst a pocoson to a corner

white oake standing by the pocoson th: N by W 76 po alonge a pocoson to
another pocoson th: along the sd pocoson NE by E ½ Ely 120 po to a
branch th: N 26 po to a Cedar branch th: NNE ½ Nly 48 po to the head of
a branch th: NNW 116 po to a corner white oake in a swamp th: NE by N
64 po to a corner pohicory th: N by E 80 po to a corner white oake by a
reedy swamp th: ENE 120 po by a line of mkd trees unto a GREAT SWAMP
th: bounding the sd swamp S ½ Wly 834 po to the first station. Sd land
being due for trans: of 14 persons: JOHN SMITH, RICHARD KEMP, JOHN
WOLFE, RICHARD WARD, MARY WORMWELL, OWEN MORGAN, WM: PINCKS (or PRICKS),
JNO: BAYMAN, EDWARD ROGERS, WM: TRUMBALL, JNO: RICHARDSON, ROBT: DAVIS,
WM: TANNER, RICHD: BAILEY.

9 Oct 1675 - RICHARD JONES SENIOR 709 acres in Lower Norfolk County
   (p584)   on the EASTWARD SIDE of ELIZABETH RIVER beginning at a
                 point on the SOUTH SIDE of LAMBERTS CREEK at an old pine
lodging upon the Point being the antient mkd tree & soe runing alongst
the MAINE RIVER S by E 44 po th: SSE 48 po th: SE by E 66 po th: SE 1/4
Sly 56 po th: S ½ Ely 38 po to a corner pine on the River th: SSE 20 po
th: S ½ Ely 52 po to a corner Mulberry tree under the Bank side th: SE
by E ½ Ely 90 po to a point on the North side of ye mouth of ELLETTS
CREEKE thence over the mouth of SANDY BRANCH CREEKE ENE 1/4 Ely 38 po
to a corner pine on the BUSHY NECK th: E ½ point Nly 36 po to a corner
pine th: ENE ½ Nly 32 po to a corner pine on a small creeke that divides
this land & ABRAHAM ELLETS thence NNE ½ Nly up the sd creeke 54 po to a
corner pine at the head of the BRUSHY NECK by a branch side th: N ½ a
point Ely 224 po to a Corner Maple in a swamp th: W by N 88 po to a corner white oake th: NW by N 100 po to a corner pine th: NNW 14 po to a
corner red oake thence NW 120 po to a corner white oake standing in the
corner of a Swamp th: SW ½ Sly 260 po to ye first station. 680 acres
of which land was formerly granted unto sd RICH: JONES by patt: dated
1 Jul 1672 & 29 acres due for trans: of one person: MARY SILKS? (This
name is at the bottom of the page and the bottom of the letters are
missing)

7 Feb 1675/6- MR ROBERT HUBBERT (*Hubert*) 168 acres 27 chaines &
   (p593)   twoe xxxxx of land in WARWICK COUNTY begin: at a stake
              adjoyning to MR. HUMPHREY HARWOODS land...............MR.
TOWNESONDS land............for trans: of fower psons: FRA: ALLETT,
ROBT: GREENE, MARY NEWMAN, & KATH: BAKER.

15 Mar 1675/6- RICHARD JONES SEGR: 200 acres in Lower Norfolk County
   (p598)   upon a Swamp called RIDGEFORD SWAMP att the head of the
                 SOUTHERNE BRANCH of ELIZA: RIVER and beginning att a mkd
tree by the swamp side being JOHN CHADWELLS corner tree and runing East
butting on the sd CHADWELLS land 229 po to a mkd oak thence North by
West 194 po butting on the land of JNO: CORPERHEW (CORPREW?) to a mkd
pine by the Swamp side being the sd CORPERHEWS corner tree thence up
the sd swamp on the severall courses thereof to the first station. For
trans: of 4 psons: MATHEW BOW, THO: LODIMORE, HERBERT JONES, MARG:
BROWNE.

15 Mar 1675/6-WM: WHITEHURST   459 acres of land in Lower Norfolk County
    (p598)   on the WEST SIDE of the INDIAN CREEK beginning att a red
                oake a corner tree of JAMES HANDSONS land & from thence
runing N by W 65 po to a corner tree of HENRY HOLSTEADS land and soe
along the sd HOLSTEADS land East 96 po to a red oak being a corner tree
of RICHARD WHITBYES land then NNW 160 po to a large mkd pine th: W by N
187 po to a mkd pine in a Swamp th: S 480 po to two small pines marked
in FADING SWAMP th: SE by E 30 po to a small mkd Spanish oak th: South
40 po to a mkd pine then East by S 74 po to a marked Red oak then East
14 po to a pine being a corner tree of THOMAS ALEXANDERS land th: East
again 16 po to JAMES HANDSONS land aforesd th: North by West 308 po by
the sd land and from th: again by that land East 79 po to the first station. For trans: of nyne psons: WM: & MARY SERSON?
THO: WATTS, HANNA WARD, ELINOR WARD, JNO: PITTMAN
Lucy & Tony negroes, LUCY TWIGAR?

15 Mar 1675/6-JNO: PRESCOTT   787 acres in Lower Norfolk County. 400
    (p598)   acres part thereof being due by a former patt: dated
                6 Nov 1665 (not in Nugent) on the EAST SIDE of the SOUTH-
ERNE BRANCH of ELIZ: RIVER bounding Southerly upon EDMOND CREEKMANS mkd
trees beginning att a mkd pine standing by a branch side & runing ESE
350 po to a mkd read oak & th: SW 210 po to a mkd pine bounding Nly upon
JNO: BIGGS his line & soe WNW 300 po to the River side & soe running by
or night (nigh?) the river side 200 po to the first station and 387 acres beeing the residue lying & joyneing to that land being bounded as
followeth vizt: begin: att a pine on a point by the branch side called
PRESCOTTS POINT & soe runing from th: by ye branch side NNE 138 po to a
mkd pine standing in ROULES? (RAWLS?) his point being a corner tree of
his former land soe runing from thence by the sd land ESE 300 po to another corner RIDG(E) by or nigh the land of JNO: BRIGGS th: SW by W 124
po to a mkd pine in LONG RIDG(E) & from th: SSW 50 po to two mkd cedars
att the branch side soe downe by the branch side WNW to the first station. Including the small points. For transportation of 8 psons: ELIZ:
HARRIS, ANN CURTIS, JNO: SHARD, Ben a negro, DANLL: NEGELTURE?, JNO:
MOORE, MARY WMS:, MARY FILCKS?

15 Mar 1675/6-EDWARD HASKELL   367 acres in Lower Norfolk County on the
    (p598)   Westerne side of the SOUTHERNE BRANCH of ELIZ: RIVER beg-
                inning at a mkd pine neere the branch side att the head
of JOSEPH MULDERS land from thence runing by the sd land NNW 200 po to
a large mkd pine th: NNE 270 po to another mkd pine hard by a gutt in
DEEPE CREEK soe up by the Creeke side W by S 210 po to another mkd pine
then S 315 po to another mkd pine then SE by E 40 po th: NE 100 po to
another mkd pine along by FRANCIS FLEETWOODS land then by the sd land
againe SE 200 po to the branch side to a mkd pine and from th: by the
branch side to the first station. For trans: of 7 persons: JNO: STONE,
BEN: BRAMBURY, MARSHALL - only name given, JNO: BRIGHT, JNO: CROSSE,
WM: COOKE, WILL: PAYNE.

15 Mar 1675/6-TIMOTHY IVES   270 acres in Lower Norfolk County on the
    (p599)   WEST SIDE of the SOUTHERN BRANCH of ELIZ: RIVER begin: at
                a mkd pine standing upon the Road point neere the mouth
of GUILLAMS RUN (Old way of spelling Williams?) and runing from thence
NNW 200 po to a cedar stump in a Marsh right against old BUTTS CREEK and
from thence WSW 320 po to a mkd poplar in a Swamp then SSE 100 po to a
marked pine then SE 21 po to a mkd white oake by GUILLAMS run and downe
by the sd run side by its severall courses including the small points
to the first station. 200 acres thereof being formerly granted unto Mr.
RICHARD JONES SEGR: by patt: dated 28 Apr 1665 and by him assigned to
TYMOTHY IVES SEGR: the 15 Feb 1671/2 as by the records of Lower Norfolk
County will appeare and by the sd TIMOTHY IVES SEGR: to his sone TIMOTHY
IVES JR: and 70 acres the remaynder being due for trans: of 2 psons:
WM: RODIMORE, ELIZ: KETCHER.

15 Mar 1675/6-RICHD: BURGESSE   332 acres in Lower Norfolk County on the
    (p599)   WEST SIDE of the SOUTHERN BRANCH of ELIZ: RIVER.   250 acres
                thereof being due by patt: dated 28 Apr 1665 to JOSEPH
MULDXX (name faded) and by him assigned to the sd BURGESSE the 19 Nov
1672 as by the Records of Lower Norfolk County may apeare and 82 acres
being the residue and bounded as followeth vizt: Marsh & woodland lying
on the EASTWARD side of the sd land in the SOUTHERNE BRANCH of ELIZ RIV-
ER aforesd runing SSW 320 po along by the land then ESE 28 po to a mkd
cedar by the branch side att the mouth of a gutt and from th: by the sd
branch side according to the severall courses thereof including all the
marsh to the first station. Said 82 acres due for trans: of 2 psons:
WM: GREENE twice.

15 Mar 1675/6-THOMAS MERCER   602 acres in Lower Norfolk County in a
    (p599)   Creeke of the SOUTHERNE BRANCH of ELIZ: RIVER called
                PUSSELL POINT (PUZZLE POINT) CREEK beginning att a mkd
white oak by the creek side then runing from thence NE 100 po to a pine
standing by a gutt side then SE 262 po th: WSW 518 po th: NNW 100 po to
a mkd beech being a corner tree of his land then againe NNW 100 po to a
mkd pine nere a Run side soe downe by the run or Creek to the first
station. 200 acres part thereof being formerly granted by patt: dated
20 Apr 1653 to RICHARD STARLING the Elder bounded as followeth: begin:
att the above mentioned white oak standing att the Creek side & soe
runing for bredth SSE 100 po to a mkd pine and soe for length WSW 320
po to a mkd beech & soe againe for bredth NNW 100 po by certaine mkd
trees to the Creek side and soe down by the Creek side ENE 320 po to the
first mentioned mkd tree & by JOSEPH NEWTONS & DENNIS MORRIS who married
the Coe heyres of the sd STARLING conveyed to MICHAELL WAYBURNES as by
their deed record(ed) in the R$_e$cords of LNco 16 Oct 1671 will apeare and
by the sd WAYBURNE conveyed to the sd MERCER by Deed recorded in ye Records of LNco afsd 17 Feb 1672/3 will also apeare & 402 acres the residue
being due for trans: of 8 psons: RICH: HARPER, JNO: GREYGOOSE, LOU BAK-
ER, PETER PORTER, JNO: SIMONDS, ALEX: ROSSE, ANTH: REBOONE, MARK LENEAR.

15 Mar 1675/6-RICHARD WHITBY 220 acres of land in Lower Norfolk County
    (p599)   in the SOUTHERNE BRANCH of ELIZ: RIVER in the County of
                Lower Norfolk on the EASTWARD SIDE of PUSSELL POINT CREEK

beginning att a mkd pine neere a gutt side being a corner tree of THOMAS
MERCERS land from thence running SE 48 po by that land to another mkd
pine then E by N 182 po to another mkd pine soe continueing that Ely
course 203 po further then NW by N 183 po to a mkd pine thence NW by
N againe 44 po to a mkd pine att the mouth of the sd Creek soe up
that Creek SW to the first station. 100 acres hereof being formerly
granted unto BARTHOLOME(W) INGOLBRITSON by pattent dated 18 Oct 1664
and by him assigned to CAPT: NICHO: & ROBT: JORDAN the 10 Feb 1664/5
and by the sd CAPT: ROBT: JORDAN assigned unto the sd RICH: WHITBY the
18 Jan 1669/70 as by the records of LNco will appeare and 120 acres the
residue being due for trans: of 3 psons: ELIZ: WHITEY, THO: BANKS,
MARY ALLEN.

15 Mar 1675/6-THEODOR(E) TAYLOR 150 acres in Lower Norfolk County in
   (p600)   the SOUTHERNE BRANCH of ELIZ: RIVER neere the head of
                JULIANS CREEK beginning at a mkd pine being JOHN WALLIS
(WALLACE?) his corner trees soe running up by the sd branch or Creeke
side NW 75 po to a mkd Red oak then NE 50 po then N 80 po then NE againe
198 po then SE 75 po then SW 198 po to a mkd pine of JNO: WALLIS his
land and by the sd land South 80 po to another pine then SW 50 po to
the first station. Sd land being part of a patt: granted RICHARD
TAYLOR & THO: NASH the 6 Nov 1665 and due to the sd THEODOR TAYLOR by
an order of the County Court of Lower Norfolk dated 17 Aug 1669. (See
1665 patent in Nugent p 565)

15 Mar 1675/6-RICHARD BACHELOR 700 acres in Lower Norfolk County. 300
   (p600)   acres part thereof being due unto the sd BACHELOR by
                severall assignmts out of a patt for 1200 acres granted
to EDWARD BROWNE & RICHARD STARNELL bearing date the 9 Mar 1658/9 (see
Nugent p 477) and some 400 acres being the remaynder lying nere the
Head of DEEPE CREEK in the SOUTHERNE BRANCH of ELIZ: RIVER in the Co.
of Lower Norf: beginning att a mkd beech standing by a Run side and being a corner tree that xxxxx his former land from the land of EDWARD
BROWNE from thence runing SSW 30 (or 38) po then NW 108 po to a mkd
beech soe continueing the said NW course 162 po further into a Swamp
then NE 192 po then SE 168 po to a mkd pine soe continueing the sd SE
course 200 po further to a mkd pine then SW 100 po downe along by the
white oak glade to a mkd gum hard by the Run side and by the Run side
& his former land to the first station. Sd 400 acres being due for
trans: of 8 psons: SARA NEEDHAM, ELIZ: NEEDHAM, JNO: THOMAS, 2 negroes,
MARGT: NEEDHAM, FRA: HARRIS, MARY BATTEN.

15 Mar 1675/6-DAVID MURRAY THE YOUNGEST 113 acres 1 rood & 6 po in
   (p602)   Lower Norfolk County in ye parish of Lynhaven called ye
                PINEY THICQUETTS (sic) on ye SOUTH SIDE of LYONS QUARTER
RUNN beginning at a corner pine on ye South side of ye sd run & runing
SSE 90 po to a corner pine thence E 72 po to a corner white oake then
SSE 56 po to a corner gum in a pocoson then SE (through?) a small pocoson 78 po to a corner red oake then NE 152 po to a corner poplar
bounding upon the Dams thence along the dams W $\frac{1}{2}$ a point Nly 66 po to a
corner beech then along ye head of ye dams WNW $\frac{1}{4}$ a point Nly 50 po to a
corner pine betwixt two runs at ye head of ye dams th: NW $\frac{1}{2}$ Nly by LIONS

QUARTER RUN 50 po to a corner white oak th: W by N towards ye head of
ye sd run 102 po to ye first station. The sd land being due unto the
sd DAVID MURRAY by and for ye trans: of 3 psons: EMANUELL DEBANNER,
ROBT: DAVISON, ANTHO: CLAUSON?

15 Mar 1675/6-MARY JOSLEN 28 acres 1 rood & 1 po in Lower Norfolk Co.
   (p602)   in the parish of Lynhaven begin: at a corner pine to-
               wards the head of a branch issueing out of BROAD CREEKE
bounding upon WM: MARTIN & ROBERT YOUNG & runing upon YOUNGS line of
mkd trees NW ½ Nly 92 po to a corner Sorrell upon BROAD CREEKE th:
SW by W 26 po to a corner pine on ye sd Creeke th: S along the sd
creeke 60 po to a corner Cedar upon the sd Creeke thence E ½ Nly 10 po
to a Corner white oake th: SSE 20 po to the mouth of a small gutt Th:
up the gutt ENE ½ Ely 52 po to a corner holy upon a Branch side then
up the Branch NE ½ Ely 14 po to the first station. The sd land being
due unto the sd MARY JOSLEN by and for trans: of one pson: THEODORE
ffLOYD.

15 Mar 1675/6-THOMAS MORRIS 200 acres in Lower Norfolk County begin:
   (p602)   at a Corner pine on the SOUTH SIDE of ye Mouth of NANNEYS
               CREEK on CURRATUCK BAY & running SSW 100 po alongst a
Marsh to a corner pine on the sd Marsh side then NW into the woods by a
line of mkd trees 320 po then NNE 100 po to ye Creeke then bounding on
the Creeke SE 320 po to the first station. For trans: of 4 psons:
THO: MORRIS, JOSIAS MORRIS, WILLIAM JOHNSON, SAMLL BROWNE.

15 Mar 1675/6-JANE BOULTON relict of WM: BOULTON decd. 350 acres in
   (p602)   Lower Norfolk County in ye woods at ye path which goeth
               from the EASTERNE BRANCH of ELIZ: RIVER to ye NORTH RIVER
begining at a mkd assh tree on ye Westerne side of a swamp thence runing SSW 194 po downe ye Swamp unto a mkd beech where the path goeth
over a run thence NW Nly along the Northeasterne side of another Swamp
unto a line of mkd trees drawne NNE 220 po unto a quarter mkd maple
tree thence from ye sd maple ESE 200 po th: SSW 140 po to the first
beginning. For trans: of 7 psons: HANNAH WHITE, THO: BROWNE, JACOB
JOHNSON twice, WM: CARLY (or CURLY), MARY MOUNT, WALTER HARMAN.

15 Mar 1675/6-SARAH RUSSELL 70 acres in Lower Norfolk County in the
   (p603)   Northerne Branches of CURRETUCK beginning at a sweet gum
               on the GREEN BRANCH and runing ENE ½ Ely by mkd trees 116
po to a dead white oake th: N by W ½ Wly 47 po to a pine th: ENE ½ Ely
60 po to a marsh that divides this land & THOMAS GRIFFINS th: SSW
bounding on the said marsh 170 po to a sweet gum then SW by S 44 po to
a sweet gum then WNW ½ Wly 28 po to a pine on the GREEN BRANCH that
divides this land and BASNETTS land then bounding on the sd branch
NNW 1/4 Wly 90 po to ye first station for trans: of 2 psons: NICHOLAS
HOFFER, HOWELL CANNAN?

15 Mar 1675/6-THOMAS MOYSER 485 acres in Lower Norfolk County lying
   (p603)   toward the head of LYNHAVEN RIVER beginning at (a) red
               oake of HENRY SMITHS & running upon his line of mkd
trees WNW 202 po to an Aish neare the BROAD RUN then WNW 1/4 Wly 164 po

to JOHN BOWRINS cleare ground th: ESE 1/4 Ely 418 po th: South 200 po
to the first station for trans: of 10 psons: THO: BROWNING, THO: GREEN,
PETER EDMONDS,RICH: RICHARDS, ALEX MARTIN, SYMON PORTER, ROGER CARDIN,
THOS: ATTWOOD, HENRY PIRTH.

15 Mar 1675/6-HENRY SPRATT 351 acres in Lower Norfolk County in the
   (p603)   parish of Lynhaven begin: at a white oake being a corner
               tree of HENRY SMITHE butting on ye Cypress Swamp & runing
upon his line of mkd trees ESE 197 po to a stooping maple then S by E
40 po to a beech then SE 38 po to a white oake thence ESE 125 po to a
poplar then SW by W 23 po to a beech at ye head of a run thence down
the run by old mkd trees dividing this land & EDMO: MOORES SSE ½ Ely
130 po to a gum on a branch of ye CYPRESS SWAMP thence downe the Branch
WSW ½ Sly 96 po to a gum thence N by W 18 po to a line of old mkd trees
thence NW by W 138 po to a gum then SW 60 po to ye Cyprus Swamp then
bounding on the sd Swamp NNW 330 po to ye first station for trans: of
7 psons: THO: WENTWORTH, JOSEPH OLIVER, WALTER HARWARR (or HARMARD?)
JNO: WOOD, JNO: POWELL, JNO: ffARIS.

6 Jun 1676 - JOHN ffREEMAN 400 acres in Lower Norfolk County neare
   (p609)   the Head of the WESTERNE BRANCH of ELIZ: RIVER begin: at
               a mkd pine being a corner tree of a pcell of land former-
ly surveyed by WILLIAM DEFNALL? and THOMAS LOVELL and running thence by
a line of mkd trees NW by N 320 po to another mkd pine th: SW by S 200
po to another mkd pine in a Swamp th: SE by E 320 po to a mkd pine on
the (inchon-nted?) ridge th: 200 po to the first menconed mkd tree
which sd land being granted to the sd JOHN FREEMAN and is due for trans:
of 8 psons: JANE? WILLIAMS, THO: EUTTE?, CHAS: MORGAN, MARY CUTTER,
RICH: REYNALDS,EDWD BROWNE, MARY HARTLY, JNO: FREEMAN. (this patent is
badly faded in spots)

1 Jun 1676 - RICHARD WHITAKER 600 acres in WARWICKE COUNTY....branch
   (p610)   of WARWICK RIVER.......butting on the land of MR. ROBERT
               CREW........land of HENRY CARY?   is part of
1058 acres granted to THOMAS BERNARD Gent by   patt: 10 Dec
1642 and purchased by sd RICHARD WHITAKER..........other 150 acres for
trans: of 3 persons. (Names not given) (This patent is badly faded)

1 Jun 1676 - CAPT: ANTHONY ARMISTEAD 928 acres in Elizabeth City Co.
   (p611)   joyning land of MARKE MORGANS orphans now in possession
               of ABRAHAM WOODWERD joyning on the severall lands of
XPHER THOMAS MOSES BAKERS orphts: & the orphan of ANTHONY TULLY? (or
SULLY?).....butting on lands of MARKE PARISH........joyning to land of
PHILLIPP JOHNSON now in possession of THOMAS JENKINS........353 acres
of said land is due sd ARMISTEAD in pte of 2 pattents. The one of 100
acres granted to THOMAS KEELING 28 Nov 1635 and thother 300 acres
granted to WILLIAM ARMISTEAD 16 May 1638 & 450 acres granted to sd
WILLIAM ARMISTED his father by patt: 7 Jul 1636 and the other 125 acres
is wast land.......due by trans: of 3 psons: HUGH JONES, JANE JONES,
THO: BOWDEN.(Thomas Keeling patent see Nugent p 34; Wm. Armistead patents see Nugent pp 45, 90, see especially p 124)

6 Jun 1676 - JOHN WELLS & EMANUELL WELLS 400 acres in WARWICK COUNTY
    (p611)   at Mulbery Island pish as by patt: bearing date 14 May
                1669 formerly granted to THOMAS IKEN and lately found to
escheat.................&c........

12 Jun 1676 - EDMD: MOORE 134 acres in Lower Norfolk County in the
    (p612)   parish of Linhaven begin: at a whiteoak neere a pocoson
                & runing E by S 92 po to a small white oak by a Swamp side
th: along the Swamp N by W 66 po to a Red oake th: NE by N 48 po to a
Spanish oake th: N 1/3 Ely 34 po to a white oak th: NE ½ Nly 116 po to
a red oake th: NW 21 po to a red oake on a pocoson th: along the pocoson SW by W ½ W 84 po to a maple th: SW ½ W 66 po to a hicory th: W ½
Nly 62 po to a Beech th: S ½ Ely 75? po to the first station for trans:
of 3 persons: WM: COOPER, JNO: MAUDEN?, ELIZ: WALLENT. (This patent is
really faded and your editor cannot vouch for accuracy in copying this
one. AGW)

12 Jun 1676 - ELIZ: BLANCH 140 acres in Lower Norfolk County on the N
    (p612)   side of DANLL: TANNERS CREEKE beginning at a Walnutt tree
                on a point dividing this land & ROBT: WOODIES & running
E ½ Sly 70 po over a Creeke to a Cedar stump on a poynt on the sd creek
dividing this land & WM: CROUCH thence NE 320 po bounding on the sd
CROUCH thence W ½ Nly 70 po th: bounding on the sd WOODIE SW 320 po to
the first station for trans: of 3 psons: JNO: GUIN (or GUM?)
TIMOTHY HOLMES, KATH: LOW.

12 Jun 1676 - ALICE PETERS 698 acres in Lower Norfolk County lying in
    (p613)   DANLL: TANNERS CREEKE begin: on a Pine on a Poynt at the
                mouth of a branch comeing out of the said creeke being a
corner tree of SAMLL: ROBERTS runing upon his line E by N 206 po to a
forked maple thence N by W by mkd trees 232 po to a pine at the head
of BOUGHS BRANCH thence bounding on the said branch WNW 64 po to a gum
on the said branch side thence W by S bounding on ye said branch 100
po to a white oake the said branch side thence W by N 126 po to a Cedar on the INDIAN TOWNE CREEKE thence WSW ½ Sly 40 po to a Cedar on ye
said creeke side thence SW by S ½ Sly 50 po to a forked Spanish oake
thence W by N 80 po to a pine on the said Creeke thence SW by W 74 po
to a pine at the mouth of ye INDIAN TOWNE CREEKE then ESE ½ Sly along
QUEEN GRAVE CREEKE 72 po to a pine thence 52 po to a white oak on the
said creeke thence ESE ½ Sly on the sd creeke 238 po to the first
station. 500 acres of which land was formerly granted to SYMON PETERS
by Patt: beareing date 20 Oct 1661 & 198 acres due for trans: of 4
persons: LEONARD WAGENER, JNO: BARNES, KATH: WELLS, THO: POMFRETT.

19 Jun 1676 - ALEXANDER FOREMAN 415 acres in Lower Norfolk County be-
    (p614)   gin: at a mkd pine being a corner tree of his former
                pattent of 400 acres dated 18 Oct 1664 & running thence
NW by N 61 po to another mkd pine thence butting on the land of MR:
RICHD: JONES W by S 169 po to a mkd gum standing on the side of a
branch called GILLAM NECK SWAMP & so along the same branches severall
courses to a mkd red oake standing alsoe on the side of the same branch

thence SE by E 132 po to a mkd gum on the Edge of a Reedy Swamp called
the CYPRESS SWAMP and soe down the said swamp to a mkd red oake anoth-
er corner tree of the said former 400 acres for trans: of 8 persons:
JNO: CLERKE, RICHD: FOREMAN, ELIZ: MATHEWS, JNO: MARTIN, RICHD: TAYLER,
SAML: JOHNSON, PETER DAWKES, AND: PACKLY. (see Nugent p 514 for 1664
patent "400 acres about 2 miles Sly from the Southerne Branch of Eliz:
River beg: in a necke formerly called the POPLAR NECKE at the CYPRESS
SWAMP".....)

___ ___ 1677 - JAMES JACKSON 200 acres being pte of a Pattent belonging
  (p621)   to JOHN GODFRY in the County of Lower Norfolk beginning
             at ye white oake branch at a marked maple tree pting it
from the land of ALEX: GWYN & from thence runing W: Northerly 200 po to
A an Ash (sic) y^ts (thats?) mkd & from thence runing No: E 160 po downe
to GATER CREEKE (Gathers Cr. ?). The said land being due for trans: of
4 persons: THOMAS TURPIN, THO: BARBER, THO: WALBROOKE, JO: BRICE.

The Umpteenth day of Oct 1677 - WARREN GODFREY 148 acres in Lower Nor-
  (p622)   folk County, land called the DAM NECKE beginning at a pop-
             lar being a corner tree of DAVID MURRAY JUN: and running
SSE by mkd trees 120 po to a gum thence SE $\frac{1}{2}$ Ely by mkd trees 130 po to
a maple thence SSW $\frac{1}{2}$ Wly 74 po to a beech thence W by N. 28 po thence S
42 po to a reedy Swampe thence bounding on the said Swampe ENE 90 po
thence on the said Swampe SE 54 po to a beech thence N 56 po to e CY-
PRESS SWAMPE thence along the CYPRESS SWAMPE NNW 30 po to the Lower
Dams thence WNW $\frac{1}{2}$ Wly 20 po thence NNW 20 po thence No: W 4U po thence
NNW 180 po to the dams thence along the Dams to the first station N $\frac{1}{2}$
Sly 92 po. For trans: of 3 psons: SARAH HODWOOD, THOMAS TAYLOR,
GEORG: TWILY?

20 Oct 1677 - WARREN GODFREY 106 acres in Lower Norfolk County joyning
  (p624)   to a tract of land called NEW DISCOVERY beginning at an
             Ash standing by a runn being a pine tree in the old Patt:
and a corner tree of WILLIAM NICHOLS and soe running SE by S bounding
on the said NICHOLLS land 210 po by marked trees to a pine thence W by
S 52 po to a beech thence NW by W 54 po to a gum thence W $\frac{1}{2}$ Nly 24 po
to a pine thence N $\frac{1}{2}$ Wly 26 po to a beech thence NW by W 44 po to a
poplar thence N by W 60 po by mkd trees to the old line thence along
the old line NE $\frac{1}{2}$ Ely 82 po to the first station for trans: of 2 psons:
WARREN GODFRY , JOHN ADKINS.

10 Oct 1678 - THOMAS ffENFORD 797 acres in Lower Norfolk County on the
  (p624)   West side of the SOUTHERNE BRANCH of ELIZ: RIVER begin:
             at the mouth of SMITHS CREEKE soe running up the branch
side E by N $\frac{1}{2}$ Nly 140 po to ffENFORDS CREEKE thence SE 160 po to a mkd
pine thence S by E 90 po to a Cedar Stump in a Marsh being the Extent
of TIMOTHY IVE(S) his land then by the said land WSW 320 po to a mkd
poplar then SSE 100 po to a mkd pine then SE 21 po to a white oake by
GWILLIAMS (This name is no doubt Williams) runn side then SW 320 po by
or nigh GWILLIAMS runn then NW 282 po thence E Nly 108 po thence

SE Eastly 150 po by JACOB SMITHS land thence NE ely 320 po to a mkd
pine thence NW Wly 150 po to a mkd beech at the head of SMITHS CREEKE
aforesaid thence downe the creek to the first station.
                200 acres being formerly granted unto RICH: KING by patt:
dated 20 Sep 1664 and by him assigned to ye sd ff.ENFORD 16 Nov 1665 as
by ye records of Lower Norfolk County & 300 acres being alsoe a part
thereof granted ffENFORD by patt: dated 21 Sep 1674 & alsoe 50 acres
hereof granted ffENFORD by patt: dated 14 7ber 1667 ye residue being
247 acres due for trans: of 5 persons: (No names given)
                (See Nugent p 493 - 200 acs to Richard King 5 Dec 1662.
this may be the above land. AGW)

18 May 1677 - JOHN ELDER 72 acres in Lower Norfolk County in ELIZA:
   (p629)   RIVER PISH begining at an old Dead oake standing by a
                branch side at the head of a Creeke and being the mkd
tree of his ancient survey from thence SE $\frac{1}{2}$ Sly 100 po by mkd trees to
a pine in a Swamp thence ENE 1/4 Ely 240 po bounding on JOHN OSBORNES
land thence 290 po to the first station. For trans of 2 persons:
ROSE RUSSELL & SARAH OWEN. (There is no patent in Nugent for John Elder)

5 Jun 1678 - RICHARD HARGRAVE JUNR: 109 acres in Lower Norfolk County
   (p635)   begin: at a white oak in COCKROFTS line & running NNE 78
                po by a line of mkd trees to a gum neare the land of
ALEXANDER GWYNS thence NW 80 po to two small pines thence ENE 86 po to
a maple thence E 86 po a white oak thence SSE 66 po to a pine thence
SW 1/4 Sly 56 po to ye orphans of HARDINGS line thence on that line WSW
140 po to the first station for trans of 2 persons: RICHARD BUCK &
JANE JNoSON:

5 Jun 1678 - RICHARD STANLEY 142 acres in Lower Norfolk County begin:
   (p636)   at a gum standing by a run Westerly from the land of
                OWEN WILLIS & running SW by W 110 po bounding on a poquo-
son to a gum thence S 40 po by mkd trees to a pine thence SW by S 114
po to a pine standing by the GREEN SEA thence SE by E 52 po to a pine
thence NE by E 158 po to a pine thence NE by N 76 po to a gum on the
said Runs thence bounding on the said run NW $\frac{1}{2}$ Nly 98 po to the first
station. The land being due by and for the trans: of 3 psons: PETER
MORELL, JNO: GORING, THO: DUKE.

5 Jun 1678 - JOHN EDWARDS 200 acres in Lower Norfolk County on the
   (p636)   Eastward side of the SOUTHERNE BRANCH of ELIZ: RIVER
                beginning at a pine being a corner tree of THOMAS ALEXAN-
DER & runing SSW by mkd trees dividing this & the said ALEXANDER 240 po
to a maple in a swamp thence ESE by mkd trees 120 po to a small poplar
in a swamp thence NNE by mkd trees 184 po to a pine thence NNW $\frac{1}{2}$ Wly
38 po to JAMES HANSONS head lyne thence W along his line 55 po to a
gumme being a corner tree of ye sd HANSONS thence along his line N by W
70 po thence to ye first station W Sly 11 po including a small ridge
of land lying Sly from his NNE line. For trans: of 4 psons: GEORGE
HORNE, ALEXANDER GETTINGS, RICHARD TIDBORNE, ELINOR BARNE.
                (See Nugent p 540 - Thomas Alexander. There is no patent
in Nugent for James Hanson)

6 Jun 1678 - WILLIAM COCKROFFT (sic)   510 acres in Lower Norfolk County
   (p636)   beginning at a Point by a branch side dividing this land
              & CHARLES EGERTON & runing NW by W $\frac{1}{2}$ Wly 112 po to a pine
at ye head of ye said branch and ye old Corner tree thence NNW 480 po
by mkd trees to a white oake thence <u>ENE of mkd trees</u> 200 po to a white
oake by a branch side being the Naturall bounds betwixt ye two ORPHANS
of THOS: HARDING thence SSW 24 po on ye sd branch thence on ye sd
branch ESE $\frac{1}{2}$ Ely 13 po to a corner tree of the division thence on the
dividing marked trees betwixt ye sd orphans SW by S 36 po thence S by
N 42 po thence S by E 16 po to ye head of a branch being the other
Naturall Bounds betwixt ye sd Orphans thence S by W 20 po on the said
branch thence on the sd branch SE by S - Sly 60 po thence E by S 100 po
thence S 1/4 Wly bounded on BROAD CREEKE 384 po to ye first station
390 acres of which land was formerly granted to THO: HARDING decd by
patt: dated 20 Oct 1661 and now due to the said COCKROFFT by marrying
one of the Orphans according to his division and 120 acres for trans:
of 2 psons: ARTHUR MOSELEY, AN MOSELEY.

29 Mar 1678/9-JOHN MATHEWS 2944 acres in WARWICK COUNTY in DENBIGH
   (p641)   PARISH......side of an old field where JNO: LEWIS lived
              ...... sd land by patt: formerly granted to SAMLL:
MATHEWS decd due to sd MR. JOHN MATHEWES as being sonn & heire to the
sd SAMLL MATHEWS decd.

2 May 1678 - JOHN TURNER (*Turner*) 1036 acres 2 rood & 32 po on
   (p643)   No side of JAMES RIVER in CHAS: CITY COUNTY in ye pish
              of WAINCOKE? ....land of LT. COLL. CLARKE on ye So:
MAJOR EDLOE on ye No:......land of MR: BRADFORD on ye East for trans:
of 21 persons: ANN BATHERS, JNO: PRICE, MARG: ELMS, SARA ASBELL,
ELIZ: ALLEN, ANN RIDER, JNO: DAVIS, GRIF: MARTERN, MARY YATES, JA: POMS,
JA: POWER, ROBT: WEBB, NORIA BRISTOLL, THO: BARTON, HEN: STINTON, ED:
PICOFT. (The names are badly faded)

5 Jun 1678 - WILLIAM COOPER 142 acres 1 rood & 18 po in Lower Norfolk
   (p647)   County lying on the SOUTH SIDE of DANIEL TANNERS CREEKE
              beginning at a pine standing on a branch called by the
name of FRESH RUN and runing W $\frac{1}{2}$ Nly 75 po to a red oake being a corner
tree of LAZARUS JENKINS thence NNE alongst a branch side 116 po to a
crooked white oake thence N 35 po on the said branch to a Creek thence
NE 56 po on the Creek thence E by S 1/4 Sly 20 po thence NE by N 35 po
thence E by S $\frac{1}{2}$ Sly 20 po thence ENE 36 po to TANNERS CREEK thence SE
12 po to ye Fresh Run Creeke thence S by W 1/4 Wly 74 po thence SW by
S 1/4 Wly 48 po thence S 1/4 Wly 84 po to the first station WSW 1/4 Wly
66 po. 42 acres 1 rood & 18 po of which land was part of a pattent
formerly granted to SAMUEL ROBBARTS dated 28 7ber 1661 and 100 acres
for trans: of 2 psons: MARY PARR, ELIZ: ALLIER.

5 Jun 1678 - JOS: WATTFORD 197 acres 3 rood & 11 po in Lower Norfolk
   (p647)   County on the SOUTH SIDE of BROAD CREEKE issueing out of
              the WESTERNE BRANCH of ELIZ: RIVER begin: on the sd Creeke
& running South by mkd trees dividing this land and the land of JNO:
WATTFORD thence N by mkd trees dividing this land and the land of RICH:

EASTWOOD to ye sd Creeke 141 po thence on the sd Creeke to ye first
station E 111 po.   50 acres of which land was formerly granted unto
THOMAS MEARES by patt: dated 1 Jun 1649 and by him assigned to JNO:
WATTFORD long since decd and being due to ye sd JOSEPH WATTFORD as heir
at law. The remainder being 50 acres due for trans: of one person:
Marie, a negro.

5 Jun 1678 - JOHN WATTFORD 97 acres 3 rood 11 po in Lower Norfolk
   (p647)   County on ye NORTH SIDE of the WESTERN BRANCH of ELIZ:
              RIVER begin: at a pine by a gutt side on the said branch
and soe runing N 141 po by mkd trees dividing this land & ROBERT BOWERS
land thence W 111 po by mkd trees dividing this land and the land of
JOS: WATTFORD thence S 141 po by mkd trees dividing this land and the
land of RICHARD EASTWOOD to the said branch thence on the sd branch to
the first station E 111 po.   50 acres of which land was formerly
granted unto THO: MEARES by pattent bearing date 1 Jun 1649 and by him
assigned to JOHN WATTFORD long since decd & becomes due to the sd JOHN
WATTFORD as heir at law. The remainder being 50 acres due for trans:
of 1 pson: Sambo 1 negroe.

5 Jun 1678 - WILLIAM POWELL 130 acres in Lower Norfolk County lying
   (p648)   at the head of a branch of LANGLEYS CREEKE on the NW side
              of the WESTERN BRANCH of ELIZ: RIVER bounded on the old
Pattent SW (scratched out in record) _E (S or N - an ink blot) 320 po
to a small white oak standing on the said branch side thence WNW 22 po
thence WSW 1/4 Sly 36 po thence SW by S 46 po thence WSW 18 po thence
W 36 po thence N 42 po by mkd trees to a white oake thence West by mkd
trees 61 po to a white oake by a pine thence to the first station
S 1/4 Ely 47 po this said land being due for trans: of 3 persons: THO:
HARDING, HENRY PULLEN, MARGARET PRITCHARD.

5 Jun 1678 - NICHOLAS HUGGINS (In the margin: "THIS PATTENT IMPERFECT"
   (p648)   and the whole patent has been crossed out) 450 acres in
              Lower Norfolk County in LYNHAVEN PARISH up the LITTLE
CREEKE against an ISLAND called HOG ISLAND begin: at the GREAT NECK
BRANCH Mouth over against HOG ISLAND next the said Creeke side and soe
runing SW bounding on the said branch to the head and from thence by
mkd trees 320 po to a maple neare COLLINS BRANCH Head thence NW 265 po
to a Spanish oake neare the dams side thence N 86 po to the dams thence
ENE downe the dams & GREAT MARSH to ye mouth thereof & from the mouth
thereof to the first station. The said land being formerly granted by
Pattents to JNO: CUBBIGE & HENRY BRAKES bearing date both the 13 Mar:
1649. (THIS PATENT PROBABLY SCRATCHED OUT BECAUSE THERE IS NO REASON
GIVEN FOR BEING DUE TO NICHOLAS HUGGINS. AGW)
              (Nugent p 187 - HENRY BRAKES 250 acres in LNco 13 Mar
1649 in Lynhaven Parish up a little creek against Hogg Island beg: at
JOHN CABBIDGES mkd tree by HOGG ISLAND CREEK side.... & Nugent p 187-
JOHN CABBIDGE 200 acres in LNco 13 Mar 1649 &c......................)

5 Jun 1678 - WILLIAM BROTHWAIT (BRAITHWAITE?) & JOSEPH MUNS 212 acres
   (p648)   in Lower Norfolk County beginning at a Hickory below MARY
              LOWES ground and running N by W by mkd trees 198 po to

the LONG PINE NECKE thence bounding on the sd Creeke SW by W towards
the head of a branch and continueing the course by marked trees 128 po
to a red oake thence W by S 34 po to a pine thence S by E 100 po to a
maple thence to the first station bounding on a Swamp E by N ½ Nly 140
po including some small points on the N by W side bounded on CHURCH
CREEKE also including the ORPHANS of LOWES land which is here to bee
excepted. For trans: of 5 psons: GEORGE PARMETER, THO: PECK, JNO:
SALMON SENR:, KATH: SALMON, JNO: SALMON JR.

9 Jun 1678 - JAMES WISHARD (modern sp. Whichard) 200 acres in Lower
   (p648)   Norfolk County neare the PINE NECK DAMS which belong to
                 LITTLE CREEKE begin: at a marked tree of ANNE BENNETTS
land standing neare the head of a branch of the said dams alsoe neare
to the HIGH ROAD from thence runing first SW by W ½ W 246 po thence
NNW 1/4 W 90 po thence NE 133 po thence ESE 1/4 Ely 170 po to the
first beginning and againe from the first beginning running first E by
N 120 po thence S by E ½ Ely 80 po thence W by S ½ Sly 108 po unto the
aforesaid dams and then up the Eastern sides of the dams unto the first
beginning which said land was formerly granted unto the said JAMES WIS-
HARD by Pattent bearing date the 8 Aug 1673 and by him deserted for
want of seating and since condemned in ye Generall Court and by order
dated 8 Jun 1678 granted unto the said JAMES WISHARD and is now due for
trans: of 4 persons: MARY MICHELL, JNO: HOLDEN, JNO: MORLE (or Merle),
JNO: WATKINS. (see page 23 of these notes)

26 Sep 1678 - ffRANCIS MASON of SURRY COUNTY inherited 300 acres of
   (p653)   land in Surry County as "heire of JNO: BISHOP decd, son
               of JNO: BISHOP decd".

27 Sep 1678 - WM: PORTEN 200 acres in Lower Norfolk County begin: at
   (p657)   a white oake being a corner tree of ye old Pattent of
               JOHN GATERS & so running E by S 400 po to a white oake
th: N by E 20 po to MR. EGERTONS corner tree then N 3/4 Wly 52 po to a
gum near GWYNS land th: W by N by mkd trees 380 (or 320) po to a neck
neare ye land of NEWMANS then S by W as part of ye old survey bounding
on ye land of NEWMAN including a small pcell of land between MR. EGER-
TONS N line & MATH: GODFREYS N by W line containing 34 acres. Due for
trans: of 4 psons: HUM: SMITH, THO: SANDWICH, ELINOR SMITH, WM:
WESTBROOKE.

24 Apr 1679 - COLL. LEMUELL MASON 1250 acres in Lower Norfolk County
   (p674)   beginning at a poynt called ye HOGPEN POYNT which lyeth
               on ye SW side of the Creeke that divides this land & ye
land of MR. THO: WILLOUGHBY & on ye East side of a branch of ye sd
Creeke near ye house of MARRACE & from thence Extendeth itself upp ye
sd Creeke Ely & Soly into a branch of ye same Creeke unto 3 marked trees
that stand at the head of a branch vist: a gum, an oake & a sassafras
& from thence S 120 po unto a mkd oake that stands on ye edge of a
GREAT PINIE SWAMP from thence W by N 320 po with mkd trees & thence
W 150 po unto a mkd oake on ye barren plaine & from thence WNW 220 po
unto 3 mkd trees vizt: a gum a oak & a pine & downe a small branch unto
ye LITTLE CREEK untill it joynes unto ye land of DOWNEMAN now in ye

tenure of Lt. ffRA: MASON & then parrellell unto ye head of DOWNEMANS
land unto ye Creeke where it began. The sd. land was by pattent dated
ye last of Aug 1642 granted to LT. ffRA: MASON father to the abovesaid
COLL: LEMUELL MASON & now new Pattented.

30 Apr 1679 - WM: GRANBERRY 85 acres in NANSEMOND COUNTY at ye head of
   (p677)   Bennetts Creek......&c..
               at lands end of ROBT: PEELES...............................

30 Apr 1679 - ROBT: PEELE SR. & ROBT: PEELE JR. (name may be Poole?)
   (p678)   175 acres in NANSEMOND COUNTY ......SAMLL GRANBERRY
               mentioned...

Note: At this point I am not sure I know how to spell my own name
correctly! Spelling used to be my "cup of tea" in school, but research
certainly undoes all that. AGW)

<u>INDEX</u>

Page numbers listed in this index refer to those of Patent Book Six.
They are listed under the date of each patent.

Notations to "see Nugent" are indexed as being on the page of Patent
Book Six on which the patent appears. They do not, however, appear in
the original patent book.

The letters "hr" indicate a headright in the patent in which the
name appears.

DEANE, Tho: hr   462
DEBANNER, Emanuell hr   602
DEBBLE, Nath: hr   242
DEFNALL ?, Wm: 609
DeHAY, Jacob hr   221
DELL, Rice hr   5
DENNES, Jane hr   286a
DENNIS, Mathew hr   584
DERIDGE, Wm: 485
DEW, Coll. Thomas   323
DEWARE, Jno: 110
DIBBLE, Nath. hr   242
DIKE, Elinor hr   464
DIRKE, Wm: hr   459
DOGHERTY, Owen hr   471
DOLLARD, Adam   221
DOOLIN, Mary hr   271
DORRINGTON, Pres: hr   489
DOTTARD, Adam   221
DOUSE, Anne hr   306
DOVELL ?, Teage et   379a
DOWIN, Tho: hr   282
DOWNEMAN, land of   674
DOWNER, Jane hr   167
DRAPER, Thomas hr   582
DRIVER, Gyles   520
DRUMMOND, William   444
DUCEING, Robt hr   306
DUELIN, Mary hr   271
DUGRAS, Nicholas hr   584
DUKE, John 452, Tho: hr   636
DUNN, ffrancis hr 584, Grace hr
     473, John hr 465
DUNNING, Tho: hr   120
DUNSCON, Robt: hr   474
DUNSTON ?, Robt: 474
DUNTON, Wm: hr   444
DURANT, Mr. George   306
DURDEN, Stephen   209
DYER, Mary & Wm: hrs   286a
                 E
EAST, Will: 477
EASTFIELD, Tho: hr   221
EASTWOOD, Rich: 647
EDCARR, Amey hr   474
EDEN, Mary hr   473
EDEY, Humphrey   337
EDICK, Sarah hr   234
EDLOE, Major   643
EDMONDS, Peter hr   603
EDWARDS, Elinor hr 464, Ellenor
     hr 419, John 636, Mary hr376

EDWARDS, William 378, Wm: hr   473
     Wm: 485, 530
EGERTON, Charles 636, Mr: 657
ELDER, John   629
ELIS, Wm: hr   472
ELLETT, Abrah: 582, Abraham   465
     584, John 242
ELLIOT, Lt. Coll. Anthony   475
     John 242, Wm: 475
ELLIS, Alice hr 474, Cornelius 532
ELLOT, John   242
ELMS, Marg: hr   643
ELWES, Tho: hr   222
EMMERSON, Hanna hr   222
EMMETT, Herbert hr   222
ENFIELD, James hr   221
ETHERIDGE, John 271, Tho: 471
EUDLING, Ja: hr   485
EUTTE, Tho: hr   609
EVANS, Tho: hr   584
EWBANKS, Henry hr   465
                 F
ffANN ?, Wm: 457
FARFITT, James   53
ffARGISON, Hugh hr   462
ffARIS, Jno: hr   603
ffARMER, Richard hr   322
ffARRELL, Geo: hr   377
FARTHINGALE, Richard   53, 352
ffEGARREL, Katherine & Morris 194
ffEGERELL, Morris hr   375
ffENFORD, Tho: 545, Thomas 222,624
FENTRIS, Jno: hr   485
ffENTRIS, Michaell   472
FERGUSON, Hugh hr 462, Hugh   528
FILCKS, Mary hr   598
ffILMER, Hen: 481
FIRTH, Mathew hr   221
ffISHER, Ann hr   485
FITZGERALD, Morris 194, hr   375
FITZGARRALL, Morris hr   528
FLEETWOOD, ffRANCIS   598
FLEMING, Christopher hr   465
FLETCHER, Mary hr   286a
FLOOD, Abraham   92
ffLOYD, Theodore hr   602
FLYNT, Capt. Thomas   218
ffOARD, Wm: hr (or fford?)   506
FOREMAN, Alexander   614
ffORGISON, Hugh   528
ffORSITH, James   352
ffORTICE, Rich: hr   453

SNEAD, Hannah hr	580	**T**	
Jeffrey hr	306	TABB, Thomas	408
SNEALE, Edward hr	47	TALBOTT, Emanuel & Rebecca hrs	286a
SNOWD (or Snowe), James hr	584	TANNER, Wm: hr	584
SOUTHERNE, Henry hr	582	TAUNTON, Robt: hr	222
SPEED, Robert hr	234	TAYLER, Richd: hr	614

SNEAD, Hannah hr — 580
    Jeffrey hr — 306
SNEALE, Edward hr — 47
SNOWD (or Snowe), James hr — 584
SOUTHERNE, Henry hr — 582
SPEED, Robert hr — 234
SPICER, Hen: hr — 472
SPIVEY, Geo: — 40
SPRATT, Hen: 472, hr 377, Mr.
    Henry 377, 603, Issabella hr
    377, Jno: hr 456
STAFFORD, Elizabeth hr — 453
STANBRIDGE, Tho: hr — 105
STANLEY, Edw. hr 485, Edwd: hr
    473, Richard 636
STANTON, Thomas hr — 322
STARLING, Richard th Elder — 599
STARNELL, Richard 110, 167, 488,
    600, (see Sternell)
STARR, Baptist hr — 304
STEGG, Ann hr — 474
STEPHENS, Thomas — 153
STERNELL, Richard — 488
STENTON, Edwd: hr — 570
STEVAN, James hr — 376
STILES, Edw: hr — 456
STINTON, Hen: — 643
STOCKMAN, Henry hr — 304
STOE, John hr 271, Thomas — 271
STONE, Jno: hr — 598
STOOKES, Robert — 209
STOUT, Tho: hr — 485
STOW, Ann, Eliz: & Isack hrs 271
    John 221, Susan hr 271
STRADLING, Ja: hr — 444
STRATFORD, Eliz: hr — 485
STRATON, Henry 477, John — 477
STRATTON, Mr. — 450
STRINGER, Anne 495, Edward hr 581
    Col. John 424, 495, Coll.
    Jno: 64
STROUD, Jo: hr — 485
STUDS, Wm: hr — 375
STURMAN, John hr — 366
SULIVANT, Daniell hr — 464
SULLY, Anthony (see Tully) — 611
SWANN, Thos: hr — 453
SWIFT, Edward hr — 286a
SWORTEN, Sara hr — 377
SYMMONDS, Robt: — 529
SYMONDS, Robt: 529, 581,
    John hr — 458

T

TABB, Thomas — 408
TALBOTT, Emanuel & Rebecca hrs 286a
TANNER, Wm: hr — 584
TAUNTON, Robt: hr — 222
TAYLER, Richd: hr — 614
TAYLOR, ffra: hr 485, Herd hr 489,
    John 458, Richard 600, hr 472,
    Theodor 600, Thomas hr 622
THARMARR, Tho: — 205
THERMAN, John hr — 254
THOMAS, Jno: hr 600, Wm: hr — 344
THOMPSON, Elizabeth hr — 528
THOMSON, Jno: hr — 361
THORLY, Roger hr — 222
THORNE, Thomas hr — 90
THORNEDON, Elizabeth hr — 105
THORNTON, Ursla hr — 581
THOROWGOOD, Adam 379, 457, 458,
    Lt. Coll. Adam 457, Major
    Adam 321, Grand Pattent of
    Mr. 458
THROWER, Jno: — 472
THRUSTON, Malachy — 408
THUCKER, Hen: hr — 306
THUMER, John hr — 209
THURMAN, John hr — 366
THURMER, John hr, 366, Robert — 24
THURSTON, Robt: hr — 105
TIDBORNE, Richard hr — 636
TIRRELL, Robert hr — 148
TITON, William hr — 90
TOLSON, Richd: hr — 485
TOM, Eliz: hr — 462
TOMLYN, Mark hr — 220
TOOLEY, Tho: 580, Thomas — 580
TOOLTON, James hr — 234
TOPPIN, Arthur 47, hr — 530
TOWMOND, Robt: — 24
TOWNESOND, Mr. — 593
TOWNSEND, Henry hr — 306
TOWNSHEND, ffrancis — 24
TRANT, Elizabeth hr — 105
TRAYLE, Robt: hr — 462
TRUMBALL, Wm: hr — 584
TRYTEN, Mich: hr — 485
TUCKER, Robert — 242
TULIES, Mr. Thomas — 306
TULLY, Orphan of Anthony — 611
TUNNELL, Tho: hr — 485
TURNER, Geo: hr 502, James 290,
    John 208, 643, Jonas hr 492,

PLACE

▼▼▼▼▼▼▼▼▼▼▼▼▼▼▼▼▼▼▼▼▼▼▼▼▼▼▼▼▼▼▼▼▼▼▼

- PLACES in LOWER NORFOLK COUNTY-